CAROL ADAMS was born in Hackney, l[...] degree in history at the University of W[...] teaching history and social studies in inner London comprehensive schools, and four years as an education officer at the Tower of London, she became, in 1980, Warden of the History and Social Sciences Teachers' Centre in London. Since 1983 she has been Inspector for Equal Opportunities for the Inner London Education Authority, working in primary and secondary schools and colleges to promote sex equality. She is married and lives in North London.

Carol Adams has always been deeply concerned with how sex roles are imposed on young women and men in our society, and how these issues are taught in schools. Her first book, the highly acclaimed *The Gender Trap* (written with Rae Laurikietis in 1976), was the first comprehensive presentation of these issues for young people. The present volume presents a non-sexist view of history. Using a remarkable combination of primary sources, oral material and contemporary photographs, *Ordinary Lives* looks at the astonishing changes in the everyday experiences of ordinary women and men over the past century. It is a unique and fascinating source book of social history for schools and colleges, as well as for the general reader.

ORDINARY
·LIVES·

A Hundred Years Ago

CAROL ADAMS

Virago

Published by VIRAGO PRESS Limited 1982
41 William IV Street, London WC2N 4DB

Reprinted 1982, 1984

Copyright © Carol Adams 1982

Typeset by Colset Limited and
Printed in Finland by Werner Söderström Oy
a member of Finnprint

British Library Cataloguing in Publication Data
Adams, Carol
  Ordinary lives.
  1. Great Britain—Social life and
  customs—19th century
  2. Great Britain—Social life and
  customs—20th century
  I. Title
  941.082   DA560
  ISBN 0-86068-239-0

Contents

Acknowledgments

My warmest thanks go to the following people who have given me so much help with the book. First and foremost to Anna Davin, who very generously made her vast and fascinating research available to me, as well as spending many evenings discussing the issues and advising me on sources and references; to Martin Davis for the illustrations and photographic reproductions; to Philippa Richardson for help with the photographic research; to my colleagues at Lewisham and Islington Green schools who tried out the material for me; to the many friends in education who read the manuscript and advised me; and to Richard Noss for all his help with editing and typing. Finally, thank you to the many people all over the country who talked to me about their memories and experiences and allowed me to quote them in the book.

PICTURE SOURCES

For kind permission to reproduce the illustrations, acknowledgements are due to the following:

Beamish North of England Open Air Museum (pp. 123, 155, 176).
Mrs Leonora Cohen (p. 217).
Fawcett Library (p. 172).

Glasgow Mitchell Library (pp. 17, 75, 81, 205).
Greater London Council Photographic Library (pp. 42, 45, 47, 50 108, 153, 160, 175, 179, 203).
Hackney Borough Council (p. 200).
Islington Libraries (pp. 22, 112).
Manchester Studies Unit at Manchester Polytechnic (p. 78).
Marie Stopes House (p. 135).
Museum of London (pp. 92, 131).
National Museum of Labour History (pp. 70, 73).
Philippa Richardson (p. 59).
Ruth Richardson (p. 186).
Salvation Army (pp. 14, 29, 36, 122, 125, 156, 173, 184, 210).
Spurgeon Collection, Greenwich Local History Library (pp. 32, 158, 202).
Weybridge Museum (pp. 18, 87, 100, 104, 127, 148, 150, 198).
Mrs M Wemyss (p. 16).

Line drawings, which appear throughout the book, are by Martin Davis

Background information

This book is intended for those studying history in school and college and for those outside education who are interested in what history is and how it is made. The book investigates what life was like for ordinary men and women living in Britain roughly a hundred years ago — that is from the 1870s until the early 1900s. In looking closely at this period, two important aspects of history are very much in evidence: those of change and difference.

CHANGE

In Britain at this time — and the book is deliberately confined to Britain — rapid changes, both technological and social, were taking place. In the 1870s there were no cars, aeroplanes, radios, films, household telephones or electricity. By 1900 they all existed or were being developed, and eventually transformed ordinary people's lives.

For the first time, too, working people were getting an education, joining trades unions, organising politically and demanding and winning the right to vote. In particular, women were beginning to fight against the restrictions of the Victorian era, and were gaining greater freedom and rights. The 1880s and 90s were marked by social upheavals which very much affect our lives today.

The material in this book explores how and why changes took place

9

between the 1870s and early 1900s. Later events are included to show further changes that have taken place over the last century – sometimes slowly and gradually, sometimes quite suddenly. Some things might not have changed as much as one might expect, nor necessarily for the better: historical change is not always the same as improvement.

DIFFERENCE

This book concentrates on ordinary people, but emphasises differences as well as similarities in people's lives. First, the different experiences of men and women are emphasised. Much written history has ignored women's lives altogether, or assumes that the history of men is the history of all people. So there is a good deal of material here about women. Then there are the differences between the social classes. There were in fact big contrasts between the lives of the very poor and the more prosperous working classes, and again between the middle classes and the very rich. This book concentrates mainly on working-class and lower-middle-class lives, but the sections on the middle and upper classes highlight some of the differences in people's experiences, according to their economic circumstances. Thirdly, there is evidence here of the differences between life in the country and the city (differences which were more marked a hundred years ago than they are today), between the north and the south, and other regions of Britain.

EVIDENCE

The book is based on evidence of various kinds. It represents the particular point of view of the writer or observer, and because it has been selected by the author it is bound to be biased and partial to some extent: all history is. There are other pieces of evidence that could have been chosen which might present a different picture. The point of examining the evidence, therefore, is to question it, to consider its context, and to compare it with other conflicting evidence where possible. There are various types of evidence included here:

Oral history: that is, interviews with people who lived at the time or who remember what they were told of it by their parents or grandparents. Most of the interviews were carried out by the author who spoke to people in many parts of the country, and these are indicated in the text. Oral evidence will, to some extent, reflect the interviewer's interests, as well as those of the person speaking.

Contemporary observations: that is, material written at the time, including magazine and newspaper articles, novels, social surveys, government reports, letters, and political speeches. These may well have been written for effect and to influence others, as in the case of a newspaper article, or they may have been more concerned with the imagination, as in the case of a novel. Often the people writing were middle-class, making value judgements on people who were working-class. Often their presence may have influenced the behaviour of the people they were observing.

Written autobiography: that is, life histories and reminiscences written after the event. In these, people present their own often highly personal interpretation of what happened, and they may only be recording what they want to remember.

Photographs: all of which were taken at the time. Some are personal, like the family portraits; some were taken for social purposes, like those of the Salvation Army. The photographer usually wanted to present a particular kind of image, and most of the subjects are posed for the photograph – they are not completely natural. Of course, the photographer had less scope to take people 'as they were' than today, because the equipment was less sophisticated.

Illustrations: based on pictures of the period from magazines and newspapers. These represent the artists' interpretation of how people and objects actually looked.

Facts and figures: such as price lists, school record books, birth and death rates. While these are as accurate as possible, they have been selected from a vast quantity of facts and figures which could be used and interpreted in different ways.

SOURCES

All the sources used are listed alphabetically by the author at the end of the book with publication dates and publishers to enable the reader to follow them up. There are other ways of investigating further the issues raised: talking to older people about their lives; reading novels and autobiographies of the period, many of which are now being published by local groups like community publishing projects; looking at collections of old photographs, which are also published locally or are available in local history libraries; looking at newspapers and magazines from the past; and examining the views and interpretations presented by historians in other books.

QUESTIONS

Some suggestions for further discussion or writing are made at the end of each chapter. These aim to raise questions about the evidence and its bias or validity, about the processes of change and about differences in time, place and economic and social position. See page 37 for note on use.

COMPARISONS

Since our money system has changed, and prices are often quoted, this conversion table will help to give some idea of what the old prices mean.

The decimal system was introduced in 1971. Before that:

One pound (£1) = 20 shillings (20/–)			
One shilling (1/–) = 12 pence or pennies (12d)			
£	s	d	p
–	1	=	½
–	6	=	2½
	1	0	=	5
	2	0	=	10
	2	6	=	12½
	5	0	=	25
	10	0	=	50
	15	0	=	75
	20	0	=	100

One guinea (£1-1s) = £1–05
Half a crown (2s/6d) = 12½p
One florin (2s) = 10p
One farthing (¼d) = –

The purchasing power of money has also changed. It's difficult to measure exactly how much real costs have changed, but, for example, in 1891:

Rent for two rooms cost	**£1-16 shillings (£1.80)**
A leather sofa cost	**£1-6 shillings (£1.30)**
Rail travel cost	**1½d a mile (½p)**
Half a dozen eggs cost	**5d (2p)**
A café lunch cost	**2/4d (13p)**
A fortnight at the seaside for a couple with two children cost	**£5.0.0**

Incomes have also changed, and with them the standard of living. There were huge differences then as now, between the incomes of the very poor, the better-off working classes, the middle classes and the very rich. As a rough guide, earnings in the 1880s would have been something like this:

CLASS	LIVING STANDARD	NUMBERS
Lower working class *(unskilled labourer, or unemployed)*	£1 per week or less 1–2 rooms frequent debts	⅓ population
Upper working class *(craftsman, clerk etc.)*	£1.10s–£2 per week half a small house just break even	⅓ population
Lower middle class *(manager, civil servant etc.)*	£3–5 per week small suburban house 1 maid	
Upper middle class *(doctor, lawyer etc.)*	£10–15 per week spacious house 2–3 servants	⅓ population
Upper class *(country landowner)*	£25 + per week large country and/or town house 6 or more servants	

East End children (1880s)

❦ 1 ❦
Growing up

Advice to parents:
'The instinct of the boy is to drum and strike in a way
that never seems to occur to his sister. He is sure to be
eager for sticks . . . while she almost as certainly cuddles
even the semblance of a child.'
Charlotte Yonge, *Womankind*, 1876

Life was hard and rough for working people in Britain at the end of the last century. From a very early age children were expected to do all they could to help their parents, in order that the family could survive, as this description of a country childhood in the 1870s illustrates:

> 'Boys fed poultry and pigs and soon were milking and cutting fire-wood. By eight years they could do much more than all that. Girls had to bath little brother and sister just a size smaller than themselves and stagger with pails of water from the tap fifty yards away when scarcely taller than the pails they carried between them. To "help" was the price of contact with beloved and admired parents; even tiny ones understood that our parents could not "manage" without us.'

> Mabel Ashby, *Joseph Ashby of Tysoe*

In working-class families girls were responsible for looking after the younger children while their mothers were busy. One writer described the girls in the East End of London in the 1880s as 'little mothers':

> 'At the open door sits a girl of eight . . . a typical "little mother" of the London doorstep . . . She is nursing a heavy baby who is perhaps a year old. She talks to it, soothes it, hushes it to sleep,

Bath night (1890s)

rocks it, dandles it when it wakes up, and kisses its poor little face again and again. But every other minute her attention is distracted by the conduct of a sister, aged four, and a brother, aged five, who are also under her guardianship . . . Because she is the oldest of all that have come, all that come after are hers to tend and hers to watch. By the time she marries and has children of her own she will be a woman weary of motherhood.'

George Sims, *How the Poor Live*

This writer, brought up at the turn of the century, describes his duties as a young boy:

'I could milk a cow by the time I was seven years old and when eight I earned sixpence a day at harvest time for "stanarding" – that is holding the horse still by its head while sheaves of corn were loaded on the cart. I would walk on at a command, then on the word "stanard" I would stop. It meant "stand hard" or still. Then at the end of the week I would line up with the men to get my pay. Most I gave to Mum to help buy boots which wore away quickly on the gritty country roads.'

George Noakes, *To be a Farmer's Boy*

16

SIX IN THE BED

Large families were common, and homes were small and crowded. This usually meant sharing not only a room but also a bed with a number of brothers or sisters. A London man, Mr Forbes, remembers his childhood in Islington in the early 1900s:

> 'We had all the boys in one bed – six of us lined up with three at the top and three at the bottom. My four sisters shared the other bed and that filled the room. There was a curtain across the middle and when my eldest sister got bigger she slept in the living room or at my aunt's nearby.'

It was quite common for older children to go and live with relatives for a while when space became a problem at home. Children were often sent out of the house to play because there just wasn't room for everyone to be in the home at once.

APPEARANCES

In most working-class families money was too scarce to buy new clothes, and only the oldest got bargains from the second-hand stall, or things made by their mothers. The younger ones wore 'hand-me-downs' which were often too big, patched and mended, and much hated. Being in fashion was simply out of the question. Photographs taken at the time show how common it was for children to play in the street and to go to school barefoot because their parents couldn't afford to buy shoes.

Children splitting sticks to make firewood, Glasgow (1910)

17

'All young boys wore dresses' (1900)

Before they started school, boys and girls had to share and swap clothes and in fact all boys including those in well-off families, wore dresses until they were 'breeched' − i.e. given their first pair of trousers at about the age of three.

> 'We were all in skirts in those days. We only started to wear knickers [trousers] when we started school, so we all looked very much alike.'
>
> **George Noakes, *To be a Farmer's Boy***

Hairstyles were a different matter. Girls usually had long hair while boys wore theirs cropped short. Grace Foakes, who grew up in the East End of London at the turn of the century, describes hers:

> 'Every Friday night at bath time my mother would wash our heads with soda, water and Sunlight soap, and then plait it into many plaits. These would not be undone until Sunday, when they were loosed, crimped and shining. My brothers went to a barber who would give them what was called a "prison crop". Every bit of hair was shaved off. This was very cold in winter but the hair took longer to grow if cut this way.'
>
> **Grace Foakes, *Between High Walls***

POCKET MONEY

In the 1880s:

One penny (½p today) would buy
¼ pound of sweets, or
a comic, or
2 icecreams

Before this century, few children got regular pocket money because their parents had little spare cash. They might have been treated to the odd farthing (a quarter of an old penny), and comics were passed around and read second-hand. The most popular fizzy drinks were lemonade and ginger beer, but many people could only afford to buy these at Christmas as a treat. In towns you could buy take-away food, and here's what one boy chose in the 1880s:

> 'I'd begin with a cup of eels, a halfpenny a cup hot, but cold, a penny, 'cos then it's fixed stiff. Eel pie is two pence, they are very good, but I'd sooner have bullocks' heart; they cost eight pence a piece; after that I think I'd have tripe, tripe and onions boiled in milk, then sheep's head or cold boiled beef, and you gets it at the shop two ounce at tuppence halfpenny. Greens is a halfpenny, and pease pudding is a halfpenny; plum pudding is a penny halfpenny a slice, but I like two "doorsteps" at a halfpenny a piece just as well.'
>
> Dorothy Tennant, 'The London Ragamuffin,'
> *English Illustrated News 1884–5*

MOTHERS AND FATHERS

Most children probably saw much more of their mothers than their fathers. Working hours were very long and by the time a man got home he was very tired or the children were in bed:

> 'My father, he didn't have a lot to do with us really. I mean he was at work all day. He was strict, strict to a certain extent but it was mother really who brought us up. My father was at work and when he used to come home it was bedtime nearly for us you see, and we didn't see a right lot of him.'
>
> Elizabeth Roberts, 'Working-Class Women in the North West'

Since working men had little time or opportunity to be involved with bringing up the family it was considered a woman's, not a man's, job. But in industrial towns many women went out to full-time work too. There were no nurseries or crêches, and babyminding was usually done by a relative or

19

neighbour — often a very young girl or an elderly woman. Because the working day was ten hours or more it was difficult for mothers to organise babyminding:

> 'I myself had some very hard times, as I had to go out to work in the mill and put the baby out to nurse. I had to get up by four in the morning, and get my baby out of bed, wash and dress it, and then leave home by five, as I had half an hour's walk to take my baby to my mother's, and then go to my work and stand all day till half past five at night and then walk home again with my baby. I had to do this with three of them.'
>
> **Margaret Llewelyn Davies (ed)** *Maternity*

Many politicians and doctors blamed working mothers for neglecting their children, believing that men should work and women should stay at home. This statement is a typical one for the times. 'For a mother to work outside the home is in every respect an individual mistake, a social tragedy, a communal blunder.' Child Welfare Conference, 1890s.

In fact many families could not survive without the mother's as well as the father's income. And this is still true of many families today.

ONE-PARENT FAMILIES

Many children lost their mother or father at an early age because people died much younger than they do today. It was very hard to bring up a family alone since there was no state scheme of financial help like social security. A mother on her own might have to get rid of her children. Here is a typical advertisement from a newspaper:

> 'ADOPTION. A good home with a mother's love and care is offered to any respectable person wishing her child to be entirely adopted. Premium £5 which includes everything. Apply by letter only.'

Such an advertisement might be for a 'baby farm' as they were called, where a poor woman made a living by looking after a number of children for money. Often things ended in tragedy if money ran short — the children could not be properly fed and died. For example, in 1870 Margaret Walters of Brixton was hanged for neglecting the children she looked after, after the bodies of sixteen babies in her care were found in one month. She had been unable to afford medical treatment or a proper burial for them.

If a mother died it was usually impossible for a father to manage alone and often the family had to go into the workhouse, or be split up among relatives. This man was helped by the local school governors:

> 'They got an old lady out of the workhouse to come and keep house for them and I think she got about half a crown [12½p] a week and

her food. If you lost your mother usually they broke your home up.'
Elizabeth Roberts, 'Working-Class Women in the North West'

NANNIES AND WET NURSES

Life was quite different if you grew up in a wealthy home — there was plenty of space, good food and clothes, and no duties to do as a child. There was always someone to look after you, but not your parents; women were hired to do this. First a 'wet nurse' was employed to breast-feed the baby in place of its natural mother. The 'ideal' wet nurse was described in a magazine in the 1870s:

'Her breath should be sweet, and perspiration free from smell; her gums firm and of good colour; teeth fine, white and perfect; she should have an abundance of milk, should have been confined [had a baby] about the same time as the mother of the child to be suckled. Her milk should be white, inodorous, inclining to a sweet taste neither watery nor thick, of moderate consistency, separating into curd over a slow fire. The age of the nurse should be from 20–35; she should be mild and sprightly, good tempered and watchful.'

The Mother's Medical Adviser

After having been breast-fed by someone else's mother, wealthy children were then brought up by a nanny in the nursery. They lived quite separately from their own parents, whom they only saw at certain times of the day. This extract describes an upper-class childhood in the 1890s:

'There was a day nursery and a night nursery and she [Nanny] was very much in charge of us. She taught us to read and write and prepared us before we went to kindergarten school. She nursed us, she looked after us. Mother at that time was very socially committed on what used to be called in those days "at home" days. Every blessed day of the week you were visiting somebody's "at home" or it was our "at home". And the church work, and so forth. Mother was out an awful lot and Nanny really, her job was to be "in loco parentis". I mean she took the load that many mothers would have carried themselves.

She really had a great deal of affection for me and if the truth be told I had perhaps more affection for my nanny than I had for my mother because I saw and lived with her and had a lot more to do with my nanny. We were very close together, she treated me almost as her own child.'

Thea Vigne, 'Parents and Children 1890–1918'

As for fathers, many children hardly saw them at all:

21

Mother and children in Islington (1890s)

'I used to see quite a lot of my mother, particularly in the mornings, and I always had to be washed and scrubbed when anyone was calling to be produced to her friends. I saw very little of my father, who used to come home from business at about six o'clock in those days and the attitude in the house was "Now, behave yourself and be quiet, your father will be very tired when he comes home and won't want you making noise." And he was very good to us as far as this world's things were concerned but he had no time at all for children, and we had, after he'd had his evening meal, to go in and say goodnight to him and kiss him, then go to bed.'

Thea Vigne, 'Parents and Children 1890–1918'

ROUGH AND READY

According to this writer, although life was hard, working-class parents did the best they could for their children:

'The children are more likely to suffer from spoiling than harshness, for they are made much of, being the pride of their mother who will sacrifice much to see them prettily dressed, and the delight of their father's heart. This makes the home and the happiness of the parents.'

Charles Booth, *Life and Labour of the London Poor*

Very young children from poor families were carried everywhere — high-chairs and prams were too expensive. Lack of space and bedding meant that babies were often taken into their parents' bed at night. This habit was often criticised on safety grounds because there were a number of baby deaths from suffocation or 'overlaying' as it was called, as a result.

There were also child deaths from fires caused by leaving oil lamps burning all night in children's rooms. When money was short, keeping the lamp on would have been a great sacrifice made by parents to comfort their child's fear of the dark, even though it was a dangerous practice. Babies got a lot of affection too from their older sisters who looked after them:

'They do not grudge the duty as a hardship, and in fact, it does not tie their movements very much, for they take the baby with them wherever they go. They have more delight in the position than their mother would probably be able to find, and, as a rule, are patient and good tempered, and unselfish, even when the baby is exceptionally tiresome.'

A. Paterson, *Across the Bridges*

Most families couldn't afford to buy a pram. Some people made them out of an old soap box and wheels, and in Bethnal Green in the 1870s they could be hired. The babies were bundled in together:

23

" EACH PRAM WAS USED TO ITS FULL CAPACITY "

'We could hire them at 1d an hour to hold one baby – or 1½d an hour to hold two. Several mothers would pay a few pence for the hire of a pram and the children used to manage between them how they were to be used. I need hardly say that each pram was used to its full seating capacity. The single pram had always to accommodate two and the double pram three or more, and we kept them for the full length of time for which we had paid. We would picnic on bread and treacle under the trees in the park and return home in the evening a troop of tired but happy children.'

Mrs Layton, 'Memories of Seventy Years',
in Margaret Llewelyn Davies (ed) *Life As We Have Known It*

'CHILDREN SHOULD BE SEEN AND NOT HEARD'

Old people's memories:
   'I once answered my mother back and she boxed my ears for it. I never did it again.'
   'You weren't allowed to chatter. If spoken to you spoke back, but having too much to say wasn't allowed.'

   In both rich and poor families, parents seem to have been strict about children's behaviour, for example, silence at meals was a common rule: only 'please' and 'thank you' were allowed. Fussiness over food was not tolerated – you had to eat everything you were given or it was served up for the next meal. There was no choice either and little variety; many children got bread and margarine or jam for most of their meals. Children were often taught to say grace – or at least in front of visitors. Maud Pember Reeves described her visit to the home of Mrs P, in London at the beginning of this century:

> 'When in the visitor's presence the little P's have swallowed a hasty dinner, which may consist of a plateful of "stoo" or perhaps a suet pudding and treacle, taken standing, they never omit to close their eyes and say "Thang Gord fer me good dinner – good afternoon Mrs R" before they go. Mrs P would call them back if they did not say that.'
>
> Maud Pember Reeves, *Round About a Pound a Week*

Adult discussions were considered unsuitable for children. Many people remember being forbidden to read the newspapers or having to leave the room when adults were talking. Children were expected to know their place in the world — after adults — and in this order of things boys came before girls. Parents may have been stricter with their daughters than with their sons, as Molly Hughes describes:

> 'My father's slogan was that boys should go everywhere and know everything and that a girl should stay at home and know nothing. The boys used to go to the theatre and music halls. Mother explained that they were not dull, only not very nice. It made no difference to me what they were like since I was never allowed to go even to a theatre.'
>
> Molly Hughes, *A London Child of the 1870s*

When it came to punishments it seems that boys were more likely to be beaten than girls. This writer vividly remembers his mother's policy:

> 'A common feature of the time was a length of leather hanging on the kitchen cupboard for the chastisement of children. "For bad boys," my mother told us, "a yard of strap is worth a mile of talk." '
>
> Robert Roberts, *A Ragged Schooling*

A minor crime could lead to harsh punishment. Grace Foakes described what happened when her brother stole a twopenny lamp:

> 'He took Robert into the bedroom, locking the door after him. He made him strip and gave him a terrible beating with the belt he wore round his waist. I shall never forget Robert's cries or my mother's tears. He was black and blue with bruises next morning . . . I do not think Robert ever forgave my father.'
>
> Grace Foakes, *Between High Walls*

CHORES

Girls had less free time than boys because they were expected to do an enormous amount in the home to help their mothers. Mrs Matthews, a Hackney woman, remembers all she had to do:

25

'Mother used to leave for night work at six in the evening. She left me to put the kids to bed and I used to do all the housework. In the morning I had to get up, get the kids ready, get the dinner ready and take the baby to the minder's all before I went to school. Most kids had to do the shopping in the morning before school – they used to send us because they served kids better than the mothers and often gave you something extra like a cake. I remember lining up in the cold for potatoes – and if you didn't do it, you didn't get your dinner. Even at nineteen you still had to do your chores before you could go out.'

Often girls were kept at home from school to help, as the school log books record:

'*17 Feb 1873*: Numbers again small . . . Parents say they would be glad to send but their daughters' services at home cannot be dispensed with.'
'*10 July 1873*: It seems almost impossible to induce the parents to make an effort to send their girls regularly – they are kept at home for everything.'

A daughter's help was especially needed on washing days:

'My fourth sister and I always stayed away from school on washing day to mind the babies. In the summer it was real sport, because so many people did their washing on the same day, and everybody had large families and generally kept the older girls, and sometimes boys, at home to mind the little ones.'

Mrs Layton, 'Memories of Seventy Years',
in Margaret Llewelyn Davies (ed) *Life As We Have Known It*

" STAYING AWAY FROM SCHOOL
ON WASHING-DAY "

ERRANDS

Boys had to do their share of housework, but they were not given full responsibility in the same way, as one man explained: 'I remember more of my sisters than my brothers. The girls were expected to look after the family and to be a mother to us and they got no peace at all.'

Boys were more likely to be given jobs to do outside the home, like running errands. In the days before telephones this might mean running for urgent help to a neighbour, or even calling out the fire brigade. Halfpenny and pennyworths of food had to be fetched each day from the local shop when people couldn't afford to buy for the whole week, and boys had to fetch beer or any other treat their parents fancied:

> 'We walked miles to satisfy the wants, whims and fancies of parents, and woe betide anyone who, having been ordered on a distant mission, makes his purchase from a shop nearer home.'
>
> **Robert Roberts, *A Ragged Schooling***

Another job was taking a hot meal to a parent or relative at work. Boys helped their fathers in the garden or allotment, chopped wood, or perhaps did the heavier jobs for their mothers, like collecting bundles of clothes for her if she took in washing.

PLAYING

Children had none of the ready-made entertainments we have today and far fewer toys, even in better-off families according to this writer:

> 'It is true that we had few toys, few magazines, few outside entertainments, and few means of getting about. But we got so much out of the few we had by anticipation, by "saving up", by exhaustive observation of the shop windows, and by the utmost use of the things we did achieve, that the well-to-do child of today can never get the same kind of pleasure.'
>
> **Molly Hughes, *A London Child of the 1870s***

They made up their own games out of everyday objects, and invented songs and rhymes. There was also less time for playing, especially for girls, as a woman teacher at the time observed: 'When the boy's school hours were over he was free to go and play with his companions. In the girl's case the home claimed her. Her playtime hours were spent in lightening her mother's labours.'

Working-class children played on the streets, which were far safer than today because there was only horse-drawn traffic − no cars. Sometimes girls and boys played separately. Skipping and hopscotch were favourites with the girls. This extract describes a game called 'Up the Buttons':

'A girl would mark a large square in chalk up near the wall of a house. They would always mark "OXO" in the centre. They then decided how many buttons each would play, say ten each. Each girl one after the other, would place ten buttons on the kerbstone, in line with the chalked square. Then they would flick each button (with the thumb and finger) forward until they all went into the square. After all the girls (say six) had flicked their buttons into the chalked square, the girl whose button was nearest or on the "X" of OXO would gather up all the buttons, 60 in all. The girls called this game "Up the Buttons".'

Albert Paul, *Poverty, Hardship but Happiness*

Boys had their own special games too, as this writer remembers:

'As the seasons changed, so did our games. Marbles, conkers, and leapfrog. As you were going to school you'd see eight to ten boys leap-frogging, one over the other until they reached the school. During the cold weather we used to swing fire cans to keep warm.'

Taffy Lewis, *Any Road*

Some games were played by everyone, and are still played today especially those based on annoying adults, like 'Knock Down Ginger' — knocking on people's doors and then running away and hiding. It was unlikely that children got away with anything more serious though, because in those days everyone in the neighbourhood knew each other and would be able to recognise a child and tell his or her parents if there was any trouble. There was one local policeman who knew all the kids and where their parents lived. A Bolton woman remembered:

'The boys congregated in groups, particularly playing football and we — the younger elements — had to be on guard for the bobby coming, because, you see, you were liable to be fined for playing football in the street in those days, you know. And so we were placed at different corners to watch out for the bobby and we used to give the call you see if we saw a bobby approaching and then of course the lads all scattered in all directions.'

Paul Thompson, 'The War with Adults'

GANGS AND VIOLENCE

On the streets, girls as well as boys had to be tough and stick up for themselves. For example, in a number of cities there was prejudice against Jewish children whose parents were immigrants, often speaking little English and living in close-knit communities. Sadie Griffiths remembers what happened in Glasgow, where she grew up at the beginning of this century:

28

'Then some of them shouted "That's the wee sheenies" and moved to kick us. We told Hilda, our older sister, to run back up the stairs – she was very timid – but my younger sister and I were not afraid. We knew they would have to run to catch us. It had happened often before. We started to run up the street – they were shouting after us, "We'll catch the wee Jews." Every kick they gave us they got one back.'

For boys, street life was tougher still. There were gangs, and racial prejudice could lead to violence in Salford:

'Syd's father in his teens belonged to the notorious mob down Cope Street. For a time the activities of this gang gained even national repute. Mr Carey, once a leader there, now looked upon himself as a model citizen. But drivelling over "happy days" he would tell of how "We stopped them bloody Yids". A Jewish dealer, we heard, had opened a secondhand clothes shop in the district, only to see his goods pulled out on the pavement and burned, while a policeman stood by to see fair play.'

Robert Roberts, *A Ragged Schooling*

WORK

Making paper streamers at home (1880s)

Although full-time work for children under twelve was illegal by the 1870s, many still worked incredibly long hours. At the bakehouse of Carr's biscuits in the 1870s children worked sixteen hours a day. The same conditions existed in many shops and workshops which were rarely visited by the few factory inspectors. In the country, many children went to straw-plaiting and lace-making 'schools' where they actually worked an eight hour day and received scarcely any education. In the northern factory towns they were allowed to work six hours a day, or twelve hours every other day in a mill and go to school part-time.

Many other children had spare time jobs – not for their own pocket money but to contribute to the family income. A survey in London schools in 1899 found that the average time an 8–9 year old boy worked was 20 hours a week, and many more did over 40 hours. Girls did mostly domestic work, as this record book from a girls' school in the 1870s shows:

NAME	AGE	OCCUPATION	HOURS PER WEEK	PAY
LC	12	housework	21	1s 6d (7½p)
MM	13	housework	34	1s 6d + food (7½p)
ED	10	errands for aunt	24	2d or 3d (1½p)
RW	10	housework and minds baby	31	1s (5p)
EC	9	errands and minds baby	30	1s (5p)
BM	11	minds a baby	39	6d + food (2½p)
GD	9	housework	27	4d (2p)
RG	10	housework and minds baby	25	6d (2½p)
KD	10	errands and minding children	37	1s 6d (7½p)
BN	12	housework and minds baby	25	6d or 9d (2½ or 4p)
JM	13	housework	19	2d + food (1p)
BM	13	minds baby	25	6d (2½p)
LH	11	housework	31	6d (2½p)

Some helped their mothers with 'homework', like matchbox making, one of the most common home industries.

> 'It is unfortunately true that homework almost invariably means child-labour – chiefly girl labour – at all hours of the day and often far into the night. Little matchbox makers work habitually from the time that school closes until eleven or even midnight.'
>
> Edith Hogg, 'School Children as Wage Earners in the Nineteenth Century', 1897

In the country they helped their mothers in the fields:

> 'We picked up acorns and sold them at a shilling a bushel and oh it did take a lot of them to make a bushel then we had to glean in the corn fields after the corn was carted and it was sent to the mill and made into flour to make us bread and then we went pea picking in the fields at 3 o'clock sometimes and then the cutting of beans.'
>
> Jenny Kitteringham, 'Country Girls in Nineteenth-Century England', in Raphael Samuel (ed) *Village Life and Labour*

Boys often worked on their own rather than help their parents. In the country they might be sent into the fields to scare away the birds at five years old. In towns they delivered papers or milk, swept crossings or cleaned shoes on the streets. There were many ways in which ingenious boys could make money. They could collect buckets of horse manure from the road and sell it at a penny a bucket (it was used as fertiliser), or hold a driver's horses for a penny while he went into a pub for a drink. Or there was selling old wood as firewood, as a London man described:

> 'Over Covent Garden with a sackful of broken-up wood, you know, flower boxes, back over Waterloo Bridge, down Tenison Street where Waterloo Station is now, knock at a door, firewood ma'am? How much? Tuppence the bagful. No, give you a penny or three halfpence. No. All right. Shoot it down the – you know – the area, and back over the Garden, four or five times, and earn about eight-pence or something like that. Used to go over Bert's, Farringdon Street, next to Earl's Corner, a packet of envelopes and paper, penny a packet, I'd sell a packet . . . in a pub – 'cos you was allowed in – we used to play on the sawdust in pubs then – back again for another – that's how we used to get hold of money. No, we never used to get anything out of our parents.'
>
> Thea Vigne, 'Parents and Children 1890–1918'

The differences in the upbringing of girls and boys affected what happened to them when they left school. A boy was quite likely to work for someone locally who had already employed him after school hours. Girls usually only had experience of domestic work, which usually paid less. This

31

A shoe-shine boy (1900)

extract from an autobiography illustrates the different prospects for girls and boys at the end of the last century:

'As soon as a little girl approached school leaving age, her mother would say, "About time you was earning your livin' me gal," or, to a neighbour, "I shan't be sorry when young so-and-so gets her knees under somebody else's table. Five slices for breakfast this mornin' if you please!" From that time onward the child was made to feel herself one too many in the overcrowded home; while her brothers, when they left school and began to bring home a few shillings weekly, were treated with a new consideration and made much of. The parents did not want the boys to leave home. Later on, if they wished to strike out for themselves, they might even meet with opposition, for their money, though barely sufficient to keep them in food, made a little more in the family purse.'

Flora Thompson, *Lark Rise to Candleford*

THE WRONG SIDE OF THE LAW

In very poor families parents were sometimes unable to look after their children, as they had to go out and work all day. There was far less provision for neglected children than there is today in terms of children's homes and social work support. A girl might drift into prostitution in order to make a living, and until 1886 the legal age of consent was only thirteen. One young girl described how she regularly went on the streets when she was left to look after the younger ones while her parents were at work. She locked the children in and went off to the West End, using the money she earned to buy food:

'I buy things to eat . . . I buy foods and give to the others what mother gives me: they don't know any better . . . sometimes we only have gruel and salt.'

W.T. Stead, *Pall Mall Gazette*, 1885

Stead, a journalist, described how he managed to buy a young girl in London in the 1880s for £5, and took her to Paris in order to show how girls were being abducted to work in brothels. He ran a campaign in his newspaper to show how easy it was for girls to be led into prostitution at a very young age. Although he was tried and imprisoned, as a result of his campaign, the legal age of consent was eventually raised to sixteen.

Boys were more likely to turn to theft for easy money, especially in the cities. This account describes Lambeth in the 1890s:

'The typical hooligan is a boy who takes to "tea-leafing" as a Grimsby lad takes to the sea. In and about Lambeth Walk we have a colony, compact and easily handled, of sturdy young villains . . .

> Life has little to give them but what they take. Honest work, if it can
> be obtained, will bring in but a few shillings a week; and what is that
> compared to the glorious possibility of "nicking a red 'un"?' [Tea-
> leafing means thieving – from cockney rhyming slang, 'tea leaf' =
> thief.]
>
> Clarence Rook, *The Hooligan Nights*

This writer found that 'tea-leafing' did not extend to the girls:

> 'She associates with criminals; but her share in crime is a passive
> one. Doubtless she suspects that the young man who takes her to
> the Canterbury and regales her on sausages and mash afterwards is
> more slippery with his hooks than behoves an honest lad. But she
> does not know or trouble her head.'
>
> Clarence Rook, *The Hooligan Nights*

A NATIONAL ASSET

By the turn of the century there was growing concern in the government
about the welfare of children. Behind it was the fear that Britain's economic
and political power in the world was being challenged by other countries,
particularly Germany. For the first time it was realised that the nation's future
depended on the children of the day. This is what some leading doctors had
to say:

> 'Now it is for us to realise fully that the future of our existence is
> wrapt up in the well-being of the children of the present.'
> 'The history of nations is determined not on the battlefield but in
> the nursery, and the battalions which give lasting victory are the
> battalions of babies.'

Now the government planned to take responsibility for the young instead
of leaving it to individual parents who, due to poverty, were unable to raise
their standards of care themselves. Boys one day would be soldiers and
workers:

> 'Whatever the primary cause . . . we are always brought back to the
> fact that the young man of 16–18 years of age is what he is because
> of the training through which he passed in his infancy and
> childhood.'
>
> Major-General Sir Frederick Maurice, 1903

Girls were a different matter; they would one day be mothers bringing up
a future generation:

> 'At the bottom of infant mortality [deaths], high or low, is good or
> bad motherhood. Give us good motherhood, and good pre-natal

34

conditions and I have no despair for the future of this or any other country.'

John Burns, trade unionist, 1901

Because of this concern, a number of Acts of Parliament were passed at the beginning of this century to reduce children's working hours, to provide more education and improve their health. For example, the 'Children's Charter' of 1908 provided school meals and health inspections and established the right of the courts to remove neglected or cruelly treated children from their parents.

Mothers too were brought into this campaign, and the first ever mothers' clinic was opened in London in 1907. This was its programme:

Consultations and weighing
Dinners for suckling mothers
Lessons on food and food values
Classes on simple cookery
Lessons on making baby clothes
Preparation for and caring for a baby
Housewifery and domestic help
Provident maternity club for saving
Fathers' evening meeting on the duties of a father
(Coffee provided and smoking allowed)

Other clinics were set up after this, and although these were small measures in view of the vast health problems and poverty faced by many families, they do show how attitudes towards children began to change.

THE WELFARE STATE

Meanwhile a growing number of voluntary and paid welfare workers, many of whom were women, were starting to campaign for stronger action that would really help the poor in a practical way, to care better for their children. Beatrice Webb and Eleanor Rathbone, for example, both worked for over 30 years to convince the government that it must provide extra money for families on low incomes. Even 30 years later things were not that different. Marjorie Soper talks about the campaign she ran with Eleanor Rathbone in the 1930s for family allowances:

'At that time all women were put down in the census as unoccupied. The Family Allowance struggle was against a background of most married women working in the home. People were beginning to talk of a minimum wage for men to cover the needs of man, wife and two

35

Queueing up for breakfast at a Salvation Army kitchen (1890s)

children. This would mean that only the man would be provided for, and it was his private affair if he spent his money on drink or gambling. It was of no interest to the state at all. A great many men wanted it to remain so and resented anything that would weaken the dependence of women on the goodwill and generosity of their husbands. A lot of opposition to Family Allowances came from the Unions. The Miners and Textile Unions were completely for it but we had to fight the others. They wanted to stick to the idea of a minimum wage for two dependent children. I wanted a state scheme to redistribute wealth so that the family got more of it when they needed it. This meant paying it to the mother directly, as hers by right to spend on the children.'

Eventually, after the Second World War ended in 1945 family allowances were introduced along with other measures such as National Insurance and the National Health Service, which have contributed to the greater welfare of children today. In addition families are now smaller and the overall standard of living in Britain has risen. All this means that more parents and children in this country have less of a hard struggle just to survive than was the case a hundred years ago. However, the gap between a poor and a wealthy childhood is still enormous. Recently the Townsend Report found that between a quarter and a third of the population live below the poverty line, that is, without enough money for an adequate standard of living. This means that some parents are still unable, for economic reasons, to feed, clothe and look after their children properly.

ATTITUDES

Attitudes, too, change very slowly. Many people still criticise mothers who work, and believe that bringing up children is a woman's rather than a man's job. There are still very few facilities like nurseries and crèches to help working parents. Boys and girls are still taught to behave differently, whether they want to or not. Compare this quote with the one at the beginning of the chapter:

> 'Sexual stereotyping starts early. To try to find out just where it starts, psychologists dressed four six-month-old babies — two boys and two girls — and presented them to eight different mothers.
>
> The children all spent half the time in pink frilly dresses and were called Jane, and the other half in blue stretch suits and were called John. The babies might not have been taken in but the mothers were. Dr Barbara Lloyd, a social psychologist at Sussex University, reported to the British Association yesterday that the first toy offered when the baby appeared as a boy was usually a hammer-shaped rattle. For a girl it was a soft pink doll. Boys were encouraged to bounce about, girls were praised for being clever and attractive. Dr Lloyd said the mothers tended to stress musculature when the baby appeared as a boy but to offer soothing activity when the girl appeared to be active. As far as Dr Lloyd and her colleagues could tell, there was no particular sex difference between the real behaviour of the actor girls and boys.'
>
> *Guardian*, September 1980

―――――――――――――――――

QUESTIONS

Note: throughout the book, questions relate to entire chapter sections; the page numbers given indicate where the relevant section starts.

A hundred years ago p. 15:

1.   What attitudes do the writers of each of these three extracts show towards children helping their parents?

2.   Based on the evidence here, would you say that children are expected to help in the same way today?

Appearances p. 17:

3.   What are the most noticeable changes in the appearance and way of life of children today compared with those in these descriptions and the photographs? Suggest reasons for these changes.

Mothers and fathers p. 19:

4.   Do you think working-class fathers saw less of their children than they do today, from this evidence?

5.   From reading the letter from *Maternity*, do you think child care was any more difficult for working mothers at this time than it is today?

6.   Why are working mothers criticised today? Why do you think they were criticised in the 1890s? Do you think the arguments for and against mothers working are different now?

One-parent families p. 20:

7.   According to the evidence here, children were adopted and families split up when a parent died. What else might have happened? What happens today?

Nannies and wet nurses p. 21 and Rough and ready p. 23:

8.   What are the most noticeable differences between a wealthy and a working-class upbringing, as illustrated by these interviews and photographs?

9.   In what ways does childhood differ today in wealthy and less well-off families? Has there been any change over the last hundred years?

'Children should be seen and not heard' p. 24:

10.   From the evidence here, and your own experience, do you think parents were stricter a hundred years ago than they are today?

11.   Why do you think there were different standards for boys and girls? Does this apply today?

Chores p. 25 and Errands p. 27:

12.   How far does the evidence indicate that boys and girls had different responsibilities? Does this apply today in your experience?

Playing p. 27:

13.   Why do you think young boys and girls often did, and still do play separately?

14.   As a child did you play any games like those described here? Which of the toys you had could have been made a hundred years ago?

Gangs and violence p. 28:

15.   Why did the children in each of these extracts feel the need to be tough? Does the same apply today?

Work p. 29:

16. Based on the evidence here, do you think children in Britain worked any harder a hundred years ago than now? Is it the same for both sexes?

The wrong side of the law p. 33:

17. Why did the young people in both of these extracts get into activities that are now in both cases illegal? Do you think the same reasons apply today?

A national asset p. 34:

18. Why was child welfare so important to the government at the turn of the century, according to the quotations here?

The welfare state p. 35 and Attitudes p. 37:

19. What were the arguments presented by Marjorie Soper for family allowances? How far do you think the state should take responsibility for children's welfare?

20. Do you think the *Guardian* report provides good evidence that girls and boys are brought up differently? Do you think that attitudes to bringing up girls and boys are changing, compared to the attitudes expressed in the quotation at the opening of the chapter?

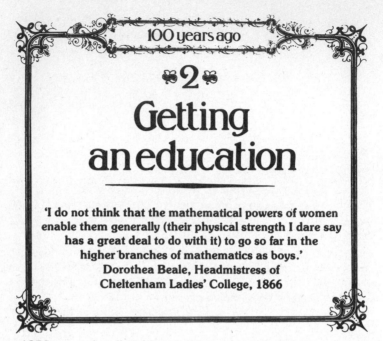

❧2❧
Getting an education

'I do not think that the mathematical powers of women
enable them generally (their physical strength I dare say
has a great deal to do with it) to go so far in the
higher branches of mathematics as boys.'
**Dorothea Beale, Headmistress of
Cheltenham Ladies' College, 1866**

From 1870 onwards, all children in Britain were supposed to go to school from the age of 5–13. By no means all children attended school regularly, but those who did attend the Board schools (the local state schools) often shocked teachers, inspectors, and visitors alike:

> 'One or two are tidy-looking boys; one has a clean, washed face and a white collar on. The rest are ragged, ill-kempt, and squalid in appearance. Some are filthy dirty, others sickly looking with sore eyes and unwholesome aspect. One or two seem hopelessly dull, almost vacant. In the girls' department it is the same. Everywhere we are met by tokens of penury [poverty] and bad conditions at home. Children are pointed to us stunted in growth, with faces old beyond their years.'
>
> **Charles Booth, *Life and Labour of the London Poor***

Many parents could ill afford to lose their children's earnings and help at home, let alone pay the school fees. (A penny to fourpence a week. This was abolished in 1891.) Some protested by attacking the teachers:

> 'I well remember how, early in my career as a teacher, I had to evade sundry missiles thrown at me by irate parents who would rather have had their children running errands and washing up things in

the home than wasting their time in school on such a thing as learning. Suppose the Education Act of 1870 had been decided by popular opinion, we should still be waiting for our schools to be built.'

'The Referendum', Women Teachers Franchise Union Pamphlet

The children were unused to the discipline of school life and the first job for the teacher was to instil some obedience and order:

'Tens of thousands of children in our schools are, I regret to say, grossly ignorant and utterly uninstructed, and the only thing we can do is to look to their cleanliness and give them habits of order, and promote their regular attendance, and then leave the question of results.'

Chairman of the London School Board, 1870

Classes were very overcrowded and noisy:

'Seventy or eighty pupils in a class are common. Sometimes there is more than one class in a room . . . many of the schools are in noisy thoroughfares . . . the teachers soon acquire the habit of shouting or, as is frequently admitted, of screaming at their pupils.'

London School Board Report, 1889

One London doctor saw so many teachers who developed bad throats from shouting that he called the complaint 'Board school laryngitis'.

" I SAID YOU WERE UNSUITABLE TO TEACH MATHS, MISS JONES ~
THE APPARATUS IS BEYOND YOUR STRENGTH. "

A London Board School class (1894)

LEARNING YOUR LESSONS

Most Board schools were mixed, with the same basic lessons for girls and boys. These were the 'Three R's' — reading, writing and arithmetic; the whole class would chant the lesson together under the teacher's instruction. This description is of a village school in the late nineteenth century:

> 'The chief business of the infants was to learn to chant the alphabet and the numbers to one hundred. In the next class they chanted tables and recited even numbers and the odd. When the children were unbearably fidgety ("fidget" was the word spoken most often by the teachers), Charlie (the teacher) would tell them to sit up straight; when he could hear a pin drop they should say their rhyme again. He would drop a pin and pretend he heard, through all the hubbub of six classes, and then the children would chant all together Charlie's own poem, waving their hands to mark the rhythm.
>
> *"Infants never must be lazy,*
> *On to work and up-si-daisy."* '
>
> Mabel Ashby, *Joseph Ashby of Tysoe*

History and geography lessons also meant learning by heart, and text-books provided set answers to be memorised. For example, a lesson on English history to be recited went like this:

'Q: Who was Henry VIII?
A: Son of Henry VII.
Q: What was his character?
A: As a young man he was bluff, generous, right royal and very handsome.
Q: How was he when he grew older?
A: He was bloated, vain, cruel and selfish.'

and so on.

NEEDLEWORK

Later schools had to introduce additional subjects to qualify for a government grant, and for these subjects girls and boys were taught separately. First, needlework was introduced for the girls. In 1873 school inspectors in London found that girls spent one quarter of school time sewing. The boys spent this extra time doing more arithmetic, which, from their point of view, seemed most unfair. Joseph Ashby remembers:

'A specially hard time was the two "sewing afternoons". While the girls were collected together for sewing, the boys merely did more sums or an extra dictation, just the sort of thing they had been doing all morning. As they craned their necks to see what sort of garments, what colours, were coming out of the vicarage basket of mending, they were unusually tiresome to the poor teacher, losing their places over and over again, or misspelling words they knew perfectly well, forgetting everything.'
Mabel Ashby, *Joseph Ashby of Tysoe*

As a result of this division, as the inspectors reported in 1878, girls could not be expected to reach the same standard in arithmetic as boys. From the pupils' point of view, needlework lessons were not always useful or practical. One woman who went to school in the 1890s remembers:

'We learnt hemming, gathering and cross-stitch. We had to practise these stitches on pieces of material, but we never learnt to make a single garment, nor to use a sewing machine.'

COOKERY

Cookery, laundrywork and domestic science soon became part of the regular curriculum for girls. The aim was to help them become better house-wives in the future, but the result was not always the desired one. One woman remembers that her efforts at cookery produced nothing but burnt offerings and rock cakes that 'really were rocks'. Another spent her laundry lessons learning how to starch white collars — but none of the men in her family wore a collar!

In the 1880s, special cookery centres were opened for girls from local schools to attend and great emphasis was placed on teaching them how to be thrifty. Girls were expected to concoct nourishing meals out of next to nothing, so that wages would stretch further. Lord Shaftesbury, like so many of the wealthier classes, believed that housewives were to blame for the poor food their families ate:

> **'I would like to see every woman of the working classes have some knowledge of cookery . . . for . . . I am certain that they are ten times less provident and more wasteful than the wealthiest in the land.'**

Here is an extract from a cookery notebook of the early 1900s; the pupil was learning how to make a thrifty but nourishing dinner:

'A dinner sufficient to feed six persons at the cost of 10d [4p] and yet containing the essentials.

Baked stuffed hearts, greens, potatoes, Semolina mould

2 baked hearts	5d
2 tsp stuffing	½d
3 tbs potatoes	1½d
Greens	½d
Semolina Mould	
1 pt milk	1½d
½ pt water	
3 tbs semolina	½d
1 tbs sugar	½d
TOTAL	**10d**

Hearts contain protein
Stuffing contains fat and carbohydrates
Potatoes contain carbohydrates
Greens contain mineral salts
Semolina mould contains fat proteins and carbohydrates'

Polytechnic of North London Archive

Learning to use a mangle in housewifery (1908)

Dishes taught in the London cookery centres 1891–2 included toad-in-the-hole, apple dumplings, Cornish pasties, mince pies, curried meat, seed cake, Christmas pudding, sausage rolls; and fig pudding. For many, these lessons were useless since their homes had no oven, or gas stove, nor the utensils necessary for making these dishes, even if there was enough money to buy the ingredients.

HOUSEWIFERY

In the 1890s housewifery centres were opened where girls spent half a day each week. This notice was displayed in these centres:

GUIDING PRINCIPLES TO ENSURE HEALTH AND HAPPINESS

a) Select a house that is thoroughly drained, well-lighted and capable of thorough ventilation.

b) Endeavour to obtain knowledge of the chief elements of food, their uses and the best method of cooking.

c) Learn the best methods of keeping your home thoroughly clean and wholesome.

d) Study how to prevent disease as well as how to restore health to those who are sick.

e) Provide recreations and amusements in the home so that the members of the family may be made happy and kept from seeking their pleasures in objectionable places.

f) Be careful and thrifty so that you may be independent in your old age

---

One woman described her visits to the centre:

'If we did the housewifery course we were taught to sweep, dust, polish, make beds and bath a life-size doll. We had great fun on this course, for it was held in a house set aside for the purpose, and with only one teacher in charge, we were quick to take advantage when she went to inspect some other part of the house. We jumped on the bed, threw pillows, drowned the doll and swept dirt under the mats. This was the highlight of the week, the one lesson we never minded going to.'

Grace Foakes, *My Part of the River*

A drawing lesson (1908)

SCIENCE

By the 1890s practical subjects were introduced for boys too – carpentry, farmwork, gardening, shoemaking, drawing, handicraft. All were aimed at training them for a job. Boys were allowed to do cookery only if they lived in seaside towns where they might get a job in catering, but it was not considered necessary for them to learn domestic skills for the home. They were educated to be breadwinners while girls were trained to be housewives.

New subjects were introduced to the higher forms of the Board schools, giving boys a far wider scope than girls. Boys could take animal physiology, physical geography, mechanics, algebra, chemistry and physics. Girls were limited to domestic economy and botany. When science was introduced in the 1890s, three times as many boys as girls attended the lessons. The reasons for teaching the subject were different for each sex:

> '. . . the relative densities of solids and liquids. For girls this knowledge is useful when testing the purity of many liquids in the household, and for boys in the detection of the alloying of metal. The course proceeds to deal with the general effects of heat upon matter.

The domestic bias in girls' education continued if they trained as 'pupil-teachers' while at school, which meant they could qualify as teachers. Girls had to pass a needlework test, while boys had to reach a higher standard of arithmetic. Girls were expected to reach the same standard in arithmetic by the end of their third year as boys were by the end of the first. At teacher training college, women could not take algebra or geometry, and did little science. Thus the skills and qualifications of men and women teachers were different, and were then passed on to their pupils.

BOOKS

There were fewer books in schools than today; reading books, called 'primers', were used. They reflect the attitudes of the times towards boys and girls, as these two extracts show:

Shan't and *Won't* were two sturdy brothers,
  Angry and sullen and gruff;
Try and *Will* are dear little sisters,
  One scarcely can love them enough.

Elder sisters, you may work,
  Work and help your mothers,
Darn the stockings, mend the shirts,
  Father's things, and brothers'.

BEHAVING YOURSELF

Most older people now remember their school days as being strict. As one woman put it: 'There was no question of cheeking the teachers in those days. What they said was law.'

Even the youngest children sat in rows — no movement or play was allowed in lessons. Most teachers had a cane, and the head of the school kept a punishment book for serious offences. Having your name in the book might mean not getting a good reference for a job when you left school, and since there were no exams like CSE or O-level, a good reference was very important. Just daring to answer back might lead to punishment; as this extract shows:

'Every Monday morning the priest came to each class, and asked us who had missed Mass the day before. I, and a few like me, always had to miss because Sunday was washing day, and we only had one lot of clothes.

So week by week we admitted our absence, and were given the strap for it. We should have been able to explain, but we just couldn't bother to make the effort, and we were ashamed to give the real reason. It was easier to come forward and get strapped on the hand instead.

Once – just once – I answered back.

"Don't you know," asked the priest, "that God loves you, and wants to see you in His house on Sundays?"

"But if He loves us, why does He want us to get the strap on Mondays if we can't go?" I asked.

I don't remember what the priest said, but I do know I got a double lot of stripes when he'd gone.'

Jane Walsh, *Not Like This*

By all accounts boys were caned far more frequently than girls. As Joseph Ashby recalls:

'It was so easy to get a beating for one thing. Some boys couldn't get through a day without "holding out their hands", or a week without a real thrashing . . . While a thrashing proceeded, the school simmered. Would a boy cry? Was the master hitting harder than usual? It might be oneself soon. The master never caned a girl, no matter how maddening she might be.'

Mabel Ashby, *Joseph Ashby of Tysoe*

Albert Paul remembers painful punishments for throwing ink pellets:

'My word, if the teacher caught any of us doing this the punishment was to kneel on the hard, rough floorboards, with your back upright and your hands placed on the back of your neck, for a long period of about 20 minutes. Should you lop over, aching all over, the teacher would slap you across the head with his hand and shout sternly "Get upright, will you?" '

Albert Paul, *Poverty, Hardship but Happiness*

It was not simply the pain that hurt, as Arthur Newton described when he was late after doing a job to help his father:

'I was kept waiting at the firm with the result that I was late. The only boy in the school to be late. I was humiliated in front of 300 boys by the Head and afterwards got six mighty slashes on the fingers with a thin cane. My God, it hurt believe me. And something else which hurt even more. My name was inserted in the disgrace and punishment book and put on record for future reference.'

Arthur Newton, Years of Change

DRILL

One method of teaching discipline, especially for boys, was military drill. Pupils were lined up in the playground to march and obey commands, as in the army. In the 1870s, teaching drill was encouraged by the government because people were uneasily aware of the impressive performance of the well-drilled Prussian army in Europe. But mainly drill was used to teach obedience in school, as one inspector recommended in the 1870s:

> 'The habit of obedience to authority, of immediate obedience to commands may tend to teach the working classes a lesson which many so sadly need in the North of England . . . submission to authority, deference to others . . . those are the real marks of manly self-respect and independence.'

Joseph Ashby described how drill was used in his class:

> 'All the children in a class came out together – or rather in order – to a series of commands. One! and you stood in your desk. Two! and you put your left leg over the seat. Three! and the right joined in.

Drill in the playground (1906)

50

Four! you faced the lane between the classes. Five! you marched on
the spot. Six! you stepped forward and the pupil-teacher chanted,
"Left, right, left, right." It was agony – you were so longing to get
outside. But if one boy pushed another you would have to go back
and begin the rigmarole again.'

Mabel Ashby, *Joseph Ashby of Tysoe*

Girls and boys were often segregated into separate playgrounds with
separate entrances. If the classes were mixed, girls and boys might be made
to sit separately and registered separately.

LOOKING NEAT AND TIDY

There was no school uniform but tidiness was encouraged, and girls seem to
have managed this better than boys because they wore pinafores over their
clothes. 'In good schools, however poor the children, they soon learn to
make themselves neat,' wrote S.E.Bray in 1900, in a report on London
girls' schools.

Albert Paul remembers his headmaster's words every Friday afternoon to
the boys:

'When you return to school on Monday morning let's have you turn
up early with your boots cleaned and a nice clean collar (and tie
straight). Also, remember, a nice clean neck and no high water
mark. (Meaning to wash your neck properly – not just down to your
collar.)'

Albert Paul, *Poverty, Hardship but Happiness*

Some teachers even imposed their standards of neatness and cleanliness
on the mothers. One London headmistress wrote in the 1880s:

'Some Christmases ago I sent a new short curtain to every house to
give it a bright appearance for Christmas Day, and now people feel a
sense of shame in various ways . . . a woman will borrow a neighbour's apron to come and speak to me so that she may come up
looking clean. I felt it my duty, if one came up to me dirty, to tell her
that she should have enough self-respect to wash her face.'

BOOTS AND DINNERS

Many headteachers in the poorest areas provided basic food and clothes for
their pupils because it was obvious that they could not learn while cold and
hungry. Many came to school without shoes, even in winter, or were kept at
home because they didn't have any. At this time there were no school
dinners or uniform grants, so it was up to each school to do something.

'Every year before the winter set in the headmaster would come in to the classrooms and ask all the boys with their fathers out of work to stand up. Lo! and behold! nearly *all* the boys would stand up. A good many boys went to school with no stockings or boots on – quite a common thing and nobody took any notice of this. They then marched up to a boot shop (named Lacey's) just above Sydney Street. We would line up on the pavement and into the shop went eight boys at a time. The assistants would fit us out with a heavy pair of hobnailed boots with metal toecaps and pelts on the heels and then as we passed out of the shop another man would punch a hole in the uppers of the boots. This prevented the parents from pawning them at the pawnbroker's.'

Albert Paul, *Poverty, Hardship but Happiness*

These are some typical school dinners in 1885:

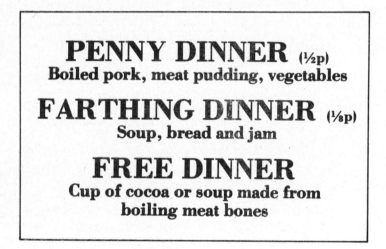

PENNY DINNER (½p)
Boiled pork, meat pudding, vegetables

FARTHING DINNER (⅛p)
Soup, bread and jam

FREE DINNER
Cup of cocoa or soup made from boiling meat bones

One visitor described the soup:

'The stomach revolts against it. It's wonderful how the teachers endure the smell.'

TRUANTING

Truancy was common. Records in London show that on average a girl missed three half-days a week; a boy only missed one half-day. Teachers noticed that many girls were away on washing day and Friday – which was a big cleaning day – and especially if there was an epidemic when they were needed to look after the sick. In the country, the school might be forced to close through poor attendance when the girls were helping with hop-picking:

The school logbook at Roxwell, Essex in 1880 records:

> **'September 19: Attempted to open school but found it impossible to do so for the girls were out gleaning and hop-picking.'**

And at Yalding in Kent in 1873,

> **'October 6: Opened school today after the Hopping Holiday. Attendance rather small, children not quite ready to come. Some are waiting to buy shoes.'**
>
> **Jenny Kitteringham, 'Country Girls in Nineteenth-Century England', in Raphael Samuel (ed)** *Village Life and Labour*

Boys were more likely to miss school when money could be earned, as at hay-making time.

This is a copy of a circular sent annually by a school board to all farmers in the district:

> Sir,
>
> I am requested by the School Board to inform you, that in case you should require any Boys for Hay-making during the present season — upon filling up and signing the Form enclosed herewith, and sending it to either of the Teachers of the Gaddesden Row Board School — the Great Gaddesden National School — or the Potten End School; leave will be given to such Boys as you may require, for a period of 4 weeks.
>
> Your obedient Servant,
> W. GROVER,
> Clerk.

While parents who sent their sons out to work were increasingly criticised by the education authorities, keeping girls at home was seen as unavoidable. As one headmistress put it:

> 'I don't see how girls are to be prevented from helping their parents . . . but a boy ought never to miss an attendance unless there is not an elder girl in the family.'

Cases of truancy might be taken to the local magistrates' court, but more boys than girls were reported, and girls were often treated more leniently. Boys truanting would be running errands or hanging about the streets, and were more likely to be found by the dreaded School Board Man whose job it was to hunt them out and report them, or the local policeman. Girls were more likely to be indoors where they could not be seen.

Girls were often allowed to leave school earlier than boys, as one inspector openly admitted: 'I should wish the boys to be kept until they have passed the fifth standard . . . and I would let the girls go when they have passed the fourth.'

Schools admitted children from three years old, but many girls had to take the babies they minded with them or miss school altogether. Some schools tried setting up crêches to encourage girls to attend, and one headteacher argued that babyrooms were as necessary as cloakrooms: 'I do not see why these babies may not be regarded as cloaks or bonnets for which provision must be made.'

Many heads simply had to allow the babies into school with their elder sisters:

> 'Children were accepted in special circumstances at the age of two-and-a-half. If the mother had a large family, or another baby was expected, then the child went to school. These children were not trained and many poor mites had to be cleaned up by the teacher. If the child had an elder sister in the school, then she would be called to clean up the child. Sometimes these babies were so tired by lunch-time that they fell asleep where they sat, much to the relief of the long-suffering teacher, I expect.'
>
> Grace Foakes, *My Part of the River*

FOR THOSE WHO COULD AFFORD IT – PUBLIC SCHOOL

Cornhill Magazine 1901:
> 'We recommend saving £300 a year from birth to send a boy to Eton, but meanwhile the girl can be kept through those twenty years for rather over £100 a year.'

Education was a very different matter for children from wealthy families. Boys and girls were far more rigidly segregated. Before this century most upper-class girls were educated at home by a governess while their brothers were sent away to boarding schools, or grammar school. Boys' schools, especially the great public schools, taught mainly the Classics — which meant Latin and Greek. Oscar Browning explained the reasons for learning these subjects, describing Eton, one of the great public schools:

> 'The tradition of interest in public affairs, of care for the reputation and honour of the Country had not died out. Classical studies did much to foster that feeling. The merit of Latin literature . . . is that it teaches the importance of human affairs, and dignity of character and conduct.'

As well as being trained for public life, boys were taught to be tough, especially through sport. W. Tuckwell described how the younger boys had to be 'fags' at cricket at Winchester:

> 'To a little boy a cricket ball swiftly bowled or swiped was as terrible as a cannon ball. The first time one came my way I deftly let it pass and ran after it. I can hear today the strident high-pitched voice of V.C. Smith, the Captain of the Eleven, whose bat had propelled it. "Fetch that ball and then come here." I stood before him, a big strong boy of nineteen or twenty. "Why did you shirk that ball?" and as he spoke he gave me a "clout" or box on the ears which knocked me down and left the glands swollen and painful for days. I have seen "middle stump" laid heavily on the loins of a little boy for the same offence.'

The fagging system, still found in many public schools today, meant that younger boys had to wait on the older ones, cleaning their shoes, cooking their breakfast and running errands; they were often cruelly treated.

ACCOMPLISHMENTS FOR YOUNG LADIES

Meanwhile their sisters' world was quite different. At home they were taught 'accomplishments' — piano playing, singing, dancing, embroidery and perhaps French conversation. These skills were considered essential for attracting a husband later on. There was no question of training for a job because middle- and upper-class women stayed at home and did not work.

There were a few small private schools for girls where the teaching was of a low standard and there was little maths and arithmetic — just as in the Board schools. In 1868, the Schools' Enquiry Commission, a government report on both girls' and boys' private schools, noted:

> 'Nothing is more common than to hear the difference in the future destiny of boys and girls assigned as a reason for the difference in the character and extent of their education. Above the age of 12, the

Advertisement for an Independent Girls' School, 1873

difference is most striking. Girls are told that Latin is not a feminine requirement, mathematics is only fit for boys, and that she must devote herself to ladylike accomplishments. I cannot find that any part of the training given in ladies' schools educates them for a domestic life, or prepares them for duties which are supposed to be especially womanly. Most girls carry away nothing but reading, an angular and scratchy handwriting, and a very indifferent skill with the needle.'

Where a fund had been set up to support both a girls' and a boys' school often the money eventually went to the boys — for example, Christ's Hospital, founded for both sexes in the sixteenth century. By the 1860s there were 1192 boys with 27 masters while the girls' school was reduced to 18 girls with one mistress. In Britain in the 1860s, £177,000 a year was spent on boys' private schools and £3000 on girls' private schools.

THE REFORMERS

From the middle of the nineteenth century, there was a growing movement among middle-class women to improve girls' education. A number of schools were opened like Cheltenham Ladies' College run by Dorothea Beale from 1858, and North London Collegiate School, founded by Frances Buss in 1850. However Dorothea Beale did not believe that a girl's education was intended to make her equal with men:

> 'I desire to institute no comparison between the mental abilities of boys and girls but simply to say what seems to be the right means of training girls so that they may best perform the subordinate part in the world to which I believe they have been called . . . for the relief of man's estate.'

But not all reformers took this view. In contrast, Emily Davies believed: 'It is difficult to see why, apart from habit, it should be good for girls to learn hemming and not good for them to learn Greek.'

To some extent, reform was limited by the views of parents who paid the fees. A typical parent would have held the view that a girl's future was marriage. Vera Brittain described her childhood at the turn of the century:

> 'In those days, as in these, girls' private schools attracted but few parents possessed of more than a half-hearted intention to train their daughters for exacting careers or even for useful occupations. Both for the young women and their mothers, the potential occurrence that loomed largest upon the horizon was marriage, and almost every girl left school with only two ambitions — to return at the first possible moment to impress her school-fellows with the glory of a grown-up toilette, and to get engaged before everybody else.'

> Vera Brittain, *Testament of Youth*

One middle-class father wrote a letter to Miss Beale opposing the teaching of arithmetic to his daughters:

> 'My dear lady, if the girls were going to be bankers it would be very well to teach them arithmetic as you do, but really there is no need.'

Shortly after this he died, leaving his daughters to manage all the family finances.

HOCKEY AND GYMSLIPS

In these new girls' schools discipline was very strict — far stricter than in boys' schools because parents needed to be sure that their daughters would be supervised and protected while away from their control. Walks were allowed only in long 'crocodiles' chaperoned by a teacher; modern novels and jewellery were banned; hair had to be tied back in plaits. Girls were strictly kept away from all members of the opposite sex, even outside the school boundaries. One girl at Oxford High School was reprimanded in the 1880s for walking in public with a boy. When she pointed out that it was her brother, the head's reply was: 'But everyone does not know it was your brother.'

Above all, silence was the golden rule.

Here are some instructions at Cheltenham College in the 1880s:

> 'Leave must be asked from the class teacher before speaking to another pupil. Leave must be obtained from both class teachers before speaking to a pupil in another class. Conversations must be finished in the place where permission is given and may not be carried on in dressing rooms, corridors or staircases.'

These were the rules at North London Collegiate School:

> 'No girl might bring a pen to school. We were forbidden to get wet on the way to school, to walk more than three in a row, to drop a pencil box, leave a book at home, run downstairs.'
>
> Molly Hughes, *A London Girl of the 1880s*

There was much emphasis on good posture, with badges awarded to those who stood with the straightest backs. In some schools girls had to lie on back boards. Games and exercise were important and many schools took up the sports played in boys' schools. Hockey, rowing, and cricket were played, and at one, even football. Sometimes sports were adapted to be easier for girls; for example softer balls were used in hockey, or underarm bowling was allowed in cricket. Girls were also hindered on the sports field by their long skirts, and not until the end of the century were shorter gym slips accepted as more practical. Vera Brittain describes the restrictions of the uniform she wore:

> 'Woollen combinations, black cashmere stockings, "liberty" bodice, dark stockingette knickers, flannel petticoat and often, in addition, a long-sleeved, high-necked, knitted woollen "spencer".
>
> At school, on the top of this conglomeration of drapery, we wore green flannel blouses in the winter and white flannel blouses in the summer, with long navy-blue skirts, linked to the blouses by elastic belts which continually slipped up or down, leaving exposed an

A school for young ladies (1890)

unsightly hiatus of blouse-tape or safety-pinned shirt-band. Green and white blouses alike had long sleeves ending in buttoned cuffs at the wrist, and high collars covering the neck almost to the chin, and fastening tightly at the throat with stiff green ties. For cricket and tennis matches, even in the baking summer of 1911, we still wore the flowing skirts and high-necked blouses, with our heavy hair tied into pigtails.'

Vera Brittain, *Testament of Youth*

UNEQUAL STILL

By the end of the century the opportunities for middle-class girls to get an education had improved. The suffragettes and suffragists, who fought for women's votes and other rights, and the pioneering work of the educational reformers, contributed a good deal to this change.

There were, however, still differences in the education provided for girls and boys. Few girls' schools had science laboratories and government grants for science education before this century all went to the boys' schools; middle-class girls did not learn domestic science because they had servants to do the housework, but they still learnt needlework. Music, singing and dancing were still common in girls' schools, but not in boys'. And in the upper and middle classes still far more boys than girls went to school. Girls made up less than a quarter of pupils in private schools at the turn of the century.

GOING TO UNIVERSITY

One reason parents may have felt it wasn't worth sending their daughters to school in the mid-nineteenth century was that they could not go to university. While boys' schools entered their pupils for the equivalent of today's 0-levels, girls could not take these before the 1860s. In 1863 Emily Davies persuaded the Oxford and Cambridge local examination boards to allow girls to sit the exams. This started a national debate. Here are some of the arguments used at the time:

> ' "There is no question that in the highest departments of original and creative power, the mind of woman is or ever can be equal to that of men." Dr Hodgson, educationalist
>
> "The examiners will favour pretty candidates." [difficult since they never saw them] – *Saturday Review*
>
> "Higher education will produce flat-chested women unable to suckle their babies." Dr Spencer, medical doctor
>
> "Giving them a boy's education will damage their reproductive organs." *The Lancet* (a medical journal)
>
> "The creation of a new race of puny, sedentary and unfeminine students would destroy the grace and charm of social life." *Contemporary Review Magazine*
>
> "There is a strong and ineradicable male instinct that a learned or even over-accomplished woman is one of the most intolerable monsters in creation." Dr Hodgson, educationalist'

By 1870, once the battle for girls to take school-leaving exams had been won, they were allowed to attend some university lectures. The first women's college, Girton College, Cambridge was established in 1874.

The college buildings were not in fact in Cambridge, but 26 miles away at Hitchen – a 'safe' distance from the men. A chaperone – an older married woman to keep an eye on the girls – was required to attend lectures with women students until 1893. They sat in the corner knitting:

> 'It is curious to look back now and see how necessary the chaperone
> was. In 1890 girls had hardly begun to walk about Oxford alone . . .
> and Oxford was particularly ready to remark on any advanced
> behaviour on the part of a woman student.'
>
> Vera Brittain, *Women at Oxford*

The behaviour of girls at university was more restricted than that of boys,
as Dora Russell remembers:

> 'You could not receive a young man in your room; you might be per-
> mitted to have him to tea in one of the public reception rooms, but
> you could accept no invitation from young men to tea or other enter-
> tainment without a chaperone from the college.'
>
> Dora Russell, *The Tamarisk Tree*

Among the middle classes, university education for a girl was considered
odd, while for a boy it was expected, as Vera Brittain found:

> 'In spite of his limited qualities of scholarship and his fitful interest in
> all non-musical subjects, the idea of refusing Edward a university
> education never so much as crossed my father's mind.
>
> The most flattering of my school reports had never, I knew, been
> regarded more seriously than my inconvenient thirst for knowledge
> and opportunities; in our family, to adapt a famous present-day
> phrase, what mattered was not the quality of the work, but the sex of
> the worker.'
>
> Vera Brittain, *Testament of Youth*

After she had applied to university, Vera Brittain's mother was asked by
her friends: 'How can you send your daughter to college, Mrs Brittain? Don't
you want her ever to get married?'

Although by the end of the century women were allowed to take all the
exams for degrees and could graduate at London and other new universi-
ties, they were not awarded degrees at Oxford until 1920: at Cambridge it
was not until 1948.

A similar struggle was fought to open medical training to women. The first
woman doctor, Elizabeth Garrett Anderson, only got on to the Medical
Register in 1865 by taking the exam for Apothecaries after private study; she
could not study at an all-male medical school. At Edinburgh, where women
were first allowed to attend some classes, they were jeered and ridiculed by
male students, and when they were finally allowed to take the exam, in
1870, the men pushed a live sheep into the examination room. Sophia Jex
Blake, who led the women's campaign at Edinburgh, started the London
School of Medicine for Women and, in 1878, London University finally

accepted women for degrees in medicine. By 1890 there were 110 registered women doctors.

Although a small minority, the women who went into higher education a hundred years ago made a great impact on society. Many became suffragettes and campaigned for women's rights; many became teachers and greatly improved the quality of girls' education; others who did not have outstanding careers, made their mark as educated, intelligent women, not prepared to go along with the old Victorian ideal of the accomplished but idle lady.

WORLDS APART

In marked contrast, secondary and higher education was an entirely closed world for all working-class children in the last century, with the very few exceptions of those who won scholarship places in grammar or private schools.

The first state secondary schools were set up after 1902, when a big expansion in secondary education for both working-class girls and boys took place. In 1897 there were only 20,000 girls attending secondary school; by 1936 there were 500,000 but this was still fewer than the number of boys – 124 girls for every 150 boys. It was intended that secondary schools should be single sex because: 'The secondary education required by girls of the industrial classes will necessarily differ in some respects from that required by boys of the same classes.' *Bryce Commission* 1894.

In fact by 1905, one in five secondary schools was mixed for reasons of economy, although the girls and boys were sometimes segregated in different parts of the building. Even in mixed schools, girls and boys were divided for some subjects; in science girls did botany and zoology while boys took physics and chemistry. And boys still received more maths teaching. A government report of 1907 recommended: 'Maths should be kept at a minimum for girls – it does not underlie their industries as it does so many of the activities of men.'

Boys and girls were separated for games and P.E., and for practical work – girls taking domestic science, while boys took woodwork and metalwork.

EDUCATION FOR LIFE

As secondary education has expanded during this century – with the raising of the school leaving-age to fourteen in 1918, fifteen in 1945 and sixteen in 1971 – more working-class children have stayed on at school to take examinations. However, schools still aim to train young people for their future lives, and in this respect there has been a continuing division between education for girls and boys. Boys are encouraged to see the most important aspect of their future as getting a job, so they are taught skills for work – craft subjects like technical drawing and metalwork. Girls are encouraged to think that being good wives and mothers is more important and they are taught skills for their future in the home, such as child-care and home economics.

Government reports on education over the last century constantly stress this division:

1874: 'A girl is not necessarily a better woman because she knows the height of all the mountains of Europe, and can work a fraction in her head; but she is decidedly better fitted for the duties she will be called upon to perform in life if she knows how to wash and tend a child, cook simple food well, and thoroughly clean a house.'

Board School Report

1904: 'The course should provide . . . Geography, History, Mathematics, Science and Drawing, with due provision for Manual Work and Physical Exercises, and, in a girls' school for Housewifery.'

Government Regulations for Secondary Schools

1943: 'Domestic science is a necessary equipment for all girls as potential makers of homes.'

The Norwood Report **on curriculum and examinations**

1959: 'With the less able girls, however, we think schools can and should make adjustments to the fact that marriage now looms much larger and nearer in the pupils' eyes than ever before.'

The Crowther Report **on education from 15–18**

1963: 'For all girls, too, there is a group of interests relating to what many, perhaps most of them, regard as their most important vocational concern – marriage.'

The Newsom Report **on pupils of less than average ability**

Since the Sex Discrimination Act of 1975, boys have been allowed by right to take domestic subjects and girls all craft subjects, but those who do so are still in the minority. Some schools have started to provide the same subjects for both sexes in earlier years – but by no means all. When it comes to pupils choosing what subjects they will take, by and large the traditional differences continue.

Girls and boys who take O- and A-levels, are supposed to have the same opportunities. However, there have always been wide variations in the

"THE HIGH-HEELED SHOE IS A FINE EXAMPLE OF THE
GREAT PRESSURE PRODUCED BY A MASS ACTING ON
A SMALL AREA ~
AS AN ARTICLE OF CLOTHING, OF COURSE, IT IS
UTTERLY STUPID."

subjects they take, and twice as many boys as girls go on to university. Girls tend to take arts subjects, especially English and foreign languages, and twice as many girls as boys study arts subjects for A-level. At O-level, over three-quarters of all candidates in physics are boys; at A-level this rises to four-fifths. This affects further training. For example, few girls take courses in engineering after they leave school because they do not have the necessary science and technical qualifications. Not surprisingly, only one in 160 graduate engineers is a woman.

The Sex Discrimination Act has, in theory, abolished the distinctions in education based on sex. In practice, as a recent report on physics textbooks illustrates, they are still much in evidence:

> 'Physics has no room for girls. That is the message of most modern physics textbooks ... physics textbooks promote a clearly masculine image for the subject and positively discourage girls from taking it. Reviewing nearly twenty books, he [the researcher] found that in pictures with people in them, men outnumbered women often by as much as ten to one.
>
> Where women were pictured, they were invariably doing something trivial, looking pretty or working at the kitchen stove rather than involved in real physics like the men.'
>
> *The Times Educational Supplement*, December 1980

QUESTIONS
A hundred years ago p. 40:

1. From these descriptions and from the photographs, how does a Board school class compare with a junior school class today? From the evidence given, what were the reasons for the children's condition, as far as you can tell?

Learning your lessons p. 42:

2. How have teaching methods with young children changed from those described on pages 42–3, and illustrated in the photograph of a classroom on p. 47? Why do you think they have changed?

3. Compare the aims of Lord Shaftesbury (p. 44) with the descriptions of cookery and housewifery lessons by ex-pupils (pp. 43–6). How far do you think the aims were realised?

4. Why did girls only do these subjects? What happens in schools you know today?

5. Do you think domestic subjects should be considered any more or any less important in schools today than they were a hundred years ago? And for boys, or girls, or both?

Behaving yourself p. 48:

6. Judging from the three extracts describing punishments, how has discipline changed today in schools you know? Is it different for boys and girls?

Drill p. 50:

7. Do we have anything similar to drill today?

Looking neat and tidy: p. 51:

8. Do schools today have more or less control over their pupils' appearances than those described here?

Boots and dinners p. 51:

9. Why did the boys described by Albert Paul need boots and school dinners? Should schools provide meals and uniforms today?

Truanting p. 52:

10. From the evidence here, do you think it was unavoidable that girls missed more school than boys?

11. Do young people truant for the same reasons today as those described here? Are the reasons the same for girls and boys?

For those who could afford it p. 54:

12. How were the aims of education different for girls and for boys among the better off? Why did a girl's education cost less?

65

13. Find out what it costs to send a boy to Eton today. Compare this to an equivalent girls' public school.

The reformers p. 57:

14. Why did parents believe a boy's education was more important than a girl's? Have these views now disappeared?

Hockey and gymslips p. 58:

15. Do you think the rules quoted were reasonable for that time?

16. Do you think there are good arguments for separate sports in schools today, or should they be mixed?

Going to university p. 60:

17. Do you think any of the arguments quoted against the idea of girls going to university were justified?

Education for life p. 62:

18. What assumptions regarding girls are made by the five government reports quoted here? Do you think these are fair assumptions? Do you agree with the policies stated?

19. The statistics given on education today indicate discrepancies between the two sexes. Do you think attitudes and opportunities are changing more than these suggest? What happens in schools you know?

20. Are there any changes you would like to see in education today?

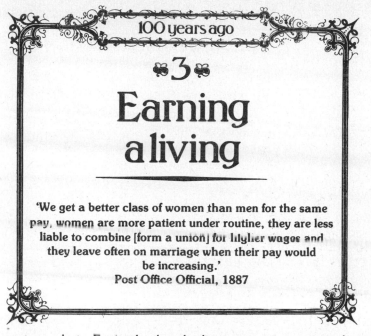

❧3❧
Earning
a living

'We get a better class of women than men for the same pay, women are more patient under routine, they are less liable to combine [form a union] for higher wages and they leave often on marriage when their pay would be increasing.'
Post Office Official, 1887

For most people in England a hundred years ago, starting work meant taking whatever job was going. A Hackney woman remembered:

> 'There was no thought of a career. I doubt if the word was ever mentioned. I got my job by the chance remark of a woman cleaner; it might have been by answering an advertisement in the *Hackney Gazette* that's how work was chosen for hundreds of poor children.'
> **Emily Bishop, 'Embroidery', *Working Lives***

The kind of work young people went into was different for girls and boys and the whole pattern of men's and women's working lives was very different. It varied of course depending on where you lived, but the outline on p. 68 gives a general idea.

A WORKING LIFE IN THE 1880s

Although women in the middle and upper classes did not usually work at the end of the nineteenth century, very few working-class men earned enough to support a family without their wives earning too. And some women were the main or only wage earners. The kind of work these women did depended on what was available locally. For example, in the cotton and wool manufacturing towns of the North many women had worked full-time in the mills since the early nineteenth century. In other areas there was little full-time work for them, and they did casual jobs. Often, work had to fit in

	MAN	WOMAN
13 years	Apprenticeship 2/6d (12½p) a week Labouring, factory odd jobs, errand boy 5/– to 7/6d (25–37½p).	Domestic service 2/6d Helper in factory 2/6d No apprenticeships. To learn a trade meant working for nothing.
14–20 years	Stay in same job, wage rises slowly: average wage £1 a week.	Change jobs often; wages much the same; promotion limited. Average wage 10/– (50p).
20–30 years (married)	Seek best work + overtime to support family; worst worries: unemployment, sickness, accident. Wages less adequate as family size increases. Average wage £1–£2 per week.	Stop work at birth of first child; jobs now temporary between births or when husband out of work. Work at home or in factory using babyminder. Wage 10–15/– (50–75p).
20–30 years (single)	Financially better off than married men. Perhaps move to find best-paid work. Live in lodgings.	Difficult to live on wage. Try to find job where board and lodging provided (e.g. domestic service).
30–40 years	Start to feel effects of overwork, e.g. less fit. Perhaps unemployed or on short time.	Work still limited by childbirth but now older children able to babymind. Support family if man sick or unemployed.
40–60 years	Perhaps disabled . . . only able to get low paid jobs. High chance of dying before 50.	Perhaps widowed or supporting family. More time to work but less fit due to many pregnancies. Wages still low.

with having a large family, so it was done at home; this included taking in washing, or sewing, or having lodgers. This kind of work was not declared on the official census returns and statistics. It was done irregularly, and was interrupted, though often only briefly, by frequent childbirth. Usually it was badly paid. But most working-class women worked. It was the pattern of their working lives and the type of work they did that distinguished their work from men's.

Working conditions were much harder for most people than today. A typical basic working week was about sixty hours – that's eleven hours a day plus a half-day on Saturday. Trade unionism was still in its very early days and workers had very few rights or protection, or control over their working conditions. There were rules and fines in most workplaces for the workers to obey, but few regulations about safety, working conditions and sufficient work breaks. By and large, a worker was at the mercy of his or her employer.

It was estimated in 1899 that for a family of two adults and three children to survive they needed about 21/– a week (£1.05p). On average, men working in towns earned just under a pound, but in the country 15/– (75p) was more common. Women's wages were, on average, half that of men's.

IN THE COUNTRY

One third of the population lived in the country in the 1880s, many of them working as agricultural labourers. It was cold, hard, dirty work, often involving the whole family, as the advertisements of the time show:

> **'WANTED: a farm labourer with a working family'**
> ### *Dorchester Chronicle*

This extract describes work at harvest time:

> **'Every man, woman and child went forth into the fields to help . . . and won the extra wage for the harvest . . . when the first corn was ready the sicklemen or scythemen with the gatherers and binders were at the field. The gatherers of the sheaves and the binders were generally the wives and children of the men and the whole work of the harvest was of the nature of a family outing . . . though a hard-working one.'**
> **David Morgan, 'The Place of Harvesters in Nineteenth-Century Village Life', in Raphael Samuel (ed) *Village Life and Labour***

Men usually did the cutting, working together as a team, while women worked with their children at gathering up the corn and gleaning (collecting all that was left over).

Flora Thompson described the women in her village:

Hop-picking (1900s)

> 'The women and children swarmed over the stubble picking up the ears of wheat the horse rake had missed . . . it was hard work from as soon as possible after daybreak until after nightfall; but the single ears mounted, and a woman with four or five strong, well-disciplined children would carry a good load home on her head every night.'
>
> Flora Thompson, *Lark Rise to Candleford*

Here is a description of men's work, written in 1889:

> 'No-one could stand the harvest field as a reaper except he had been born to it . . . their necks grew black . . . their arms tough as ash, seemed cased in leather. They grew visibly thinner in the harvest field and shrunk together – all flesh disappearing and nothing but sinew and muscle remaining. Never was such work . . . so they worked and slaved and tore at the wheat . . . the heat, the aches, the illness, the sunstroke always impending in the air.'
>
> Richard Jeffries, *Field and Hedgerow*

Much of the women's work was done by hand, and included weeding and hoeing, gathering and trimming vegetables. It was done in the open fields and in all weathers:

'There are degrees of dampness and a very little is called being wet through in common talk. But to stand working slowly in a field, and feel the creep of rainwater, first in the legs and shoulders, then on hips and head, then at back front and sides, and yet to work on 'til the leaden light diminishes and marks that the sun is down, demands a distinct modicum of stoicism, even valour.'

Thomas Hardy, *Tess of the D'Urbervilles*

While farmwork was hard, many people remember its pleasures too. Beer was provided for thirsty harvesters; there were picnics in the fields, the advantages of working outside in fine weather, and the comparative freedom from the eye of the boss as in a factory.

'UNLADYLIKE'

Towards the end of the century, a big increase in imported food meant fewer jobs in agriculture. Women were laid off first, and one of the reasons given for no longer employing them was that farmwork was 'immoral' or indecent because men and women worked together in the fields. The following extract is from a government investigation:

'That which seems most to lower the moral or decent tone of the peasant girls is the sensation of independence of society which they acquire in the fields.'

Another criticism in this report was that women would tuck their skirts up to keep them out of the way when working in the fields:

" YOU MEAN POTATOES ACTUALLY GROW UNDERGROUND ?!!
DON'T THEY GET DIRTY ? "

> 'They turn up their dresses to their waists and walk about with their legs bare . . . when the crops are wet, they tuck up their dresses between the legs, often leaving the legs much exposed.'

Even worse than showing an ankle was 'answering the calls of nature':

> 'The long absence and distance from home often render it necessary that the women should attend to the calls of nature and this they frequently do in the presence of lads, boys and men.'
>
> Report on the Employment of Children, Young Persons and Women in Agriculture 1868–9

New farming machinery was also introduced by the 1880s, notably the reaping machine for cutting corn, which was only worked by men. As a result, by the end of the century, it had become less common for women to work on the land. Flora Thompson summed up the changes in farm work in her village:

> 'A few women still did field work, not with the men, not even in the same field as a rule but at their own special tasks. Formerly, it was said, there had been a large gang of field women – slatternly creatures . . . their day was over; but the reputation they had left behind them had given most country women a distaste for "goin' afield". In the eighties, about half-a-dozen of the hamlet women who, having got their families off hand, had spare time, a liking for the open-air life and a longing for a few shillings a week they could call their own.'
>
> Flora Thompson, Lark Rise to Candleford

HEAVY WORK

As more machinery was introduced, the skilled, better-paid work was increasingly restricted to men. However, many women still did jobs that contradicted all ideas of what was 'feminine and ladylike'. In the salt works in Cheshire, for example, where whole families still worked together, the man depended on the help of his wife and children to earn a decent wage. Women made up 40 per cent of the workforce, combining the work with child care and running the home.

> 'Groups of weary women and sleepy-eyed children made their way through the pitch darkness to the wych house. The lumpman, their husband or employer, would already be at work preparing for the first of the day's "droughts" or boilings . . . When the salt had been made, each lump had to be carried to the stove and stood upright in the ditches. Each lump weighed about 45 lbs while the salt was still wet and the women had about 50–70 of these to move in quick succession. As soon as the salt was safely in the stove, the women

would return home to prepare breakfast and begin their household tasks. In a little over two hours, working in total darkness and intense heat and strength-sapping humidity, each woman had shovelled, shaped and carried about a ton of salt.'

Brian Didsbury, 'Salt Workers', in Raphael Samuel (ed) *Miners, Quarrymen and Saltworkers*

This family earned about £1 a week altogether. Because of the humidity, the women's loose clothing clung to their bodies, which led to complaints by the inspectors of 'immorality':

'The supposed tendency to promote immorality arises in this way . . . in "drawing" [taking the salt from the pan] the women wear a shift not always closely fastened at the neck, and a petticoat. Often men are moving about the same pan, perfectly naked from the waist up. Owing to the heat and the moisture, such clothes as are worn, instead of concealing, cling to and emphasise the figure. That is, when the mist lets you see any figure at all.'

Superintending Inspector's Report 1878

WEARING THE TROUSERS

Some women in dirty jobs, like mining, wore trousers, for which they were severely criticised by both employers and male workers. As the introduction of machinery led to fewer jobs all round, women in these dirty, heavy jobs were increasingly under attack.

The Miners' Union Conference at Leeds in the 1860s declared:

Chain making at Cradley Heath (1906)

'It is a most sickening sight to see girls and women who had been created and designed for a much nobler sphere of action, clad in men's attire on the pit banks.'

The *Daily News* reported:

'Trousers are a disgusting kind of male attire that completely unsexes women, rendering them in most respects exceedingly repulsive.'

Earlier in the century women had been banned from working underground in coal mines, but many still worked at the surface, and also at the brickworks found on many coalfields.

'I found the girls at work making bricks in a low shed having no windows or opening for the admission of light except for the doorway through which I entered . . . They temper it with their bare feet, moving rapidly about the clay and water reaching to the calf of the leg. This operation completed, they grasp with both arms a lump of clay weighing about 35 lbs and supporting it upon their bosoms they carry this load to the moulding table where other girls, with a plentiful use of cold water, mould it into bricks. They have to feed and attend to the furnaces used for heating the floors in the open air, exposed to the vicissitudes of the weather and the changes of temperature alternating between the heat of the drying room and the cold outside.'

Morning Chronicle, 1886

A woman brickworker told A.J. Munby:

'I reckon myself as strong as a man, for lifting and everything and a sight stronger than some of the men too and I works as hard as they. Yes, I can make bricks as well as any man – I should think so.'

Derek Hudson, *Munby, Man of Two Worlds*

She made five hundred bricks an hour for 2/– (10p) a day.

Often women workers fought against the government's efforts to prevent their doing heavy work. For example, a group of women chainmakers from Cradley Heath, in 1887, came to see the Home Secretary to protest against the proposal to prevent their working the heavier hammers, for health reasons:

'As soon as they got into the room, the Home Secretary began to explain to them that a certain important medical officer had reported to him that the heavier hammers would be prejudicial to their health, especially those who were of child-bearing age. A very stalwart-looking woman immediately exclaimed "I ha' had fourteen

Ironworkers (1890s)

children sir, and I never was better in my life." The Home Secretary expressed polite satisfaction, and again quoted the doctor, whereupon all the nail and chainmakers exclaimed in chorus, "He's dead, sir," as much as to say, "He's dead and we're alive so we needn't bother about him any more." '

Ray Strachey, *The Cause*

As a result they were successful in stopping the restrictions which would have limited them to the lower paid work.

In the cities, rough dirty jobs were often done by women as well as by men. There were dustwomen whose work in those days included collecting manure left by horses in the streets, female mudlarks who waded in the river to collect stray coals from the barges, and milkwomen, who carried the milk in pails across their shoulders on a yoke. Often the worst-paid and dirtiest jobs were done by Irish women who could get no other work. The Irish were discriminated against because they were new immigrants, poor, and poorly educated. Arthur Munby described a milkwoman:

'She walked thus away between her heavy cans, her mother keeping her at her side and guiding her to the next customer on the milk walk. Doubtless she felt happy, when after being hired she was sent to the coopers to fit herself with a new yoke. Doubtless when she

75

first walked along the streets this afternoon, she felt proud of wearing a new yoke with big letters on it . . . long may she feel such pride. She will work in that year out of doors six hours a day, in all weathers, with never a holiday from year's end to year's end.'

Derek Hudson, *Munby, Man of Two Worlds*

DANGEROUS JOBS

However, there was very little concern or government interference in the conditions of men's work. In mining the introduction of the Davey safety lamp meant that new and deeper seams could be dug and this increased the risk of accident. In the 1870s, 1000 miners were killed every year. One Durham miner remembers his working conditions:

'The thin seams of Durham are a nightmare and many's the nightmare I've had about them since . . . Crawling down the seam, only inches would separate the roof from your prostrate body, your head would be turned to the side, flat against the floor with maybe a two inch space above you before you made contact with the roof. Crawling was called "belly flopper"; you would "swim" forward arms straight out in front, legs spread-eagled behind, pushing, striving, wriggling forward, and always the roof, bumping and creaking inches above your head.'

Dave Douglass, 'Pit Life in County Durham',
in Raphael Samuel (ed) *Miners, Quarrymen and Saltworkers*

Ironmaking was another job fraught with danger in the hand-worked blast furnaces of the 1890s:

'The path of the ironworks is literally strewn with danger, for as he walks along, the innocent-looking fragment, no longer glowing, may be a piece of hot iron of which the touch, if he stepped on it, is enough to cripple him; one splash of the molten steam may blind him; if he were to stumble as he walks along the edge of that sandy platform where the iron is bubbling and rushing into the moulds he would never get up again.'

Lady Florence Bell, *At the Works*

Not only was the work hard and a constant strain, but terrible accidents happened, like this one, in the 1880s:

'Three years ago one of the most terrible of all accidents occurred, in which two men fell into one of the blast-furnaces. The bell, the metal cone already described, on to which the charge is put before it is lowered into the furnace, was being changed, and the old bell was being lowered into the furnace. As it was lowered some accidental contact produced an explosion, and a man who was standing regulating its descent on a plank fastened to the side of the furnace fell off into the glowing mass beneath, where the temperature is about 3,000 degrees F. Another who was with him on the plank, who had retained his footing, absolutely lost his head, helplessly stepped forward and met the same fate. A third, who was nearer the side of the furnace, was seized, and managed, half-dazed, to scramble out, after living through the moment in which the same fate might have overtaken himself, although not through what must have been the wild and unimaginable agony of his fellows in that second before they became unconscious.'

Lady Florence Bell, *At the Works*

This work was relatively well-paid at 25–38/– a week (around £1.50p.). While it was only men who had to risk their lives like this, their jobs very much affected their wives as well. There was no state help for a family which had lost its breadwinner. A miner's wife, in the days before pithead baths, had endless hard work in preparing baths and washing black clothes by hand, for a husband and perhaps several sons. Shift work demanded being woken and having to prepare food at all hours, as well as the constant worry that this time the breadwinner would not return home at all.

FACTORY WORK

Throughout the last century, the number of jobs in factories was growing. Men and women worked side by side, but they did different jobs for different wages. In many factories, men earned twice as much as women.

Courtauld's silk factory in Essex illustrates the division between men's and women's jobs:

JOB	WAGE	NO. OF MEN	NO. OF WOMEN
Weaver	5–8/– (25–40p)	0	589
Winder	2–6/– (10–30p)	38	188
Overseers and Clerks	15–32/– (75p–£1–60p)	26	0
Machinery Attendants	10–15/– (50–75p)	34	0

Courtauld Register of Employees, supplied by Judy Lown

Employers justified the division of work by saying that men and women

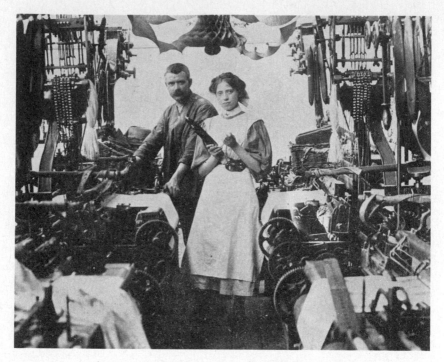

A weaver and loom overlooker, Bolton (1909)

had different skills and aptitudes. For example, one employer described women as follows: 'They are more orderly, quieter and neater, they meet with no accidents and exert an influence in checking the rude language and jesting of the men. They have a neatness of touch rather than power of touch.'

This meant that they did light work by hand instead of better-paid work with machinery.

Men working in factories or workshops could learn a skill by serving an apprenticeship, and for them there was more likely to be some satisfaction in the job itself:

> 'In those days a man's work, though more laborious to his muscles, was not nearly so exhausting yet tedious as machinery and "speeding-up" have since made it for his mind and temper. "Eight hours" today is less interesting and probably more toilsome than "twelve hours" then.'
>
> George Sturt, 'A Wheelwright', in John Burnett (ed), *Useful Toil*

78

RULES AND REGULATIONS

Factory life was strictly controlled. In 1888 at the Bryant and May match factory in East London, girls were fined out of their week's wages of 4/– (20p) as follows:

3d (1½p) for leaving their work area dirty **1/– (5p) for putting burnt-out matches on the bench** **3d (1p) for talking**

Other fines commonly imposed in factories were for sneezing: 1d (½p), reading: 1/– (5p), bad language: 1/– (5p), laughing and making a noise: 1d (½p).

Young girls were closely supervised. Flo Mellish remembers:

> 'The first time I ever worked in Fry's, I had to go into a room and learn the way to cover chocolate. And I'm telling you, that was queer. For three days I had someone to teach me. And at the end of that time I had to go on piece work. It was to cover little creams which were called tens. We used to have to cover 120 for three farthings. A couple of weeks after they put it up to a penny. I didn't like it and I didn't get on very well and I really wanted to leave. But of course you couldn't leave. You had to work where you were sent, there was mother at home waiting for the money.
>
> We daren't talk, and we daren't laugh. If we laughed or if we talked we had to leave off. She'd tell you, "Leave off and sit". We had to sit on our stools and wait half an hour. And then we'd start work again. I took home one week 2/10d.'
>
> **Flo Mellish,** *Bristol As We Remember It*

At Courtauld's factory, women employees were dismissed for having an illegitimate child, living with a man unmarried, or bad behaviour at work. The management criticised men for drunkenness and wasting their earnings that should have been spent on their families, but they were not generally dismissed for this behaviour. Courtaulds tried to control all aspects of their women employees' lives; there were classes for them in child care, a lodging house for single girls, and an Amusement Society, which however allowed no drink or music. Attempts were made to influence men's behaviour, but not to the same extent.

In spite of strict rules about behaviour, factory girls had a reputation for being rowdy, confident and cheerful, and enjoying the financial independence and social life that work offered, even if it was dreary. One writer, Alys Russell, described their behaviour in the streets:

'The instant the bell went at five-thirty there was a bolt for the mess room, and the girls were dressed in hat and jacket and out in the street almost before the bell had stopped. Those girls who lived in my direction walked with me until I was so tired that I had to get into a 'bus; Clara, my "mate", on one arm, pretty Lizzie, with her ear-rings and bold bright eyes, on the other; several other girls rollicking in front, a few more straggling behind. They were in riotous spirits, and pulled an occasional door bell as we passed along, and shouted at every man we met. They saw me into my 'bus with many "good-nights", which they repeated with redoubled shouts and laughter as a little later they drove past the 'bus in the open cart of some kind waggoner.'

Alys Russell, 'Four Days in a Factory',
Contemporary Review, July 1903

THE SWEATED TRADES

Work done at home or in small workshops for a contractor or 'middle-man' was called 'sweated work'. It was poorly paid on a piece-work basis (that is, according to the amount done). Often it was done under the worst condi-tions, as this description of London in the 1890s shows:

'In a room perhaps 12 or 14 feet by 10 and some 8 feet high we find several girls and women packed together, stitching without a moment's pause, or working sewing machines on heavy cloth gar-ments, while the tailor heats irons at a gas or coke fire and presses the seams, filling the air with steam; or it is a fur pulling shop, and the air is filled with dust and hairs; or a boot closers or umbrella-makers and the smell of sour paste, old leather and old cloth and all the refuse of a trade is added to the smell and litter of ill-kept family life; for, too often, the room in which the trade is carried on is that in which the family eats and sleeps also.'

Miss March-Phillips, 'The Evils of Home Work for Women', in
Investigation Papers, Women's Co-operative Guild, 1898

The wages for this work might be as low as 3/− (15p) a week. Often there was a glut of work at particular times of the year − for example, during the 'season' when ladies ordered new dresses − followed by unemployment for months. Ladies' magazines often urged readers to be more thoughtful towards their poor dressmakers, who had to work all hours to finish orders taken at the last minute. In 1908 girls worked from 8.00 one morning until 4.00 the following afternoon to get gowns finished for Ascot. In 1843, Thomas Hood published the 'Song of the Shirt' on the plight of sewing women. At the end of the century it might well have been sung by women earning their living at a sewing machine:

Winding bobbins in an attic workshop, Glasgow (1890)

'With fingers heavy and worn
With eyelids heavy and red,
A woman sat in unwomanly rags
Plying her needle and thread:
Stitch! stitch! stitch!
In poverty hunger and dirt,
And still, with a voice of dolorous pitch
She sang the "Song of the Shirt".

Work-work-work
'Til the brain begins to swim;
Work-work-work
'Til the eyes are heavy and dim;
Seam and gusset and band
Band and gusset and seam
'Til over the buttons I fall asleep,
And sew them on in my dreams!

Oh men, with sisters dear
Oh men with mothers and wives,
It is not linen you're wearing out
But human creatures' lives.
Stitch! stitch! stitch!
In poverty hunger and dirt,
Sewing at once with a double thread
A shroud as well as a shirt.'

Some women were driven to prostitution because of the low wages. In the 1860s, Henry Mayhew interviewed women earning 2½d (1p) per shirt 'finishing' seven shirts a week:

> ' "I went to the streets solely to get a living for myself and my child. If I had been able to get it otherwise I would have done so . . . It was the low price paid for my labour that drove me to prostitution."
>
> She believed that all women in her job were forced into prostitution:
>
> "I never knew one girl in the trade who was virtuous. Most of them wished to be so but were compelled to be otherwise for mere life." '
>
> Henry Mayhew, *London Labour and the London Poor*

Prostitution was better-paid than most women's jobs, according to this 'price list' from the 1880s:

> '£1 . . . for a very good woman
> 10/– (50p) . . . for as nice a woman as you needed
> 5/– (25p) . . . for quite a nice girl
> A silk pocket handkerchief for a poor girl. (This could be sold for 3–4/– – more than a week's wages.)'
>
> Walter, 'My Secret Life', in Stephen Marcus,
> *The Other Victorians*

'Sweated' work for men meant casual labour, like dock work. Here too they were paid by a contractor according to the work available and this fluctuated giving long periods of short-time work or unemployment. In the 1880s there was an economic depression with increased unemployment, so there were more men in need of work than there were jobs. It was a humiliating battle to get taken on as James Gray, a dock labourer, told the Select Commons Committee of 1888:

> 'At half past eleven I should say there was something like 350 men waiting for employment at this special gate. A contractor by the name of Clemence came to the gate for, I think it was 14 men; it was either 14 or 16 and of course there was a struggle . . . It is a common occurrence for men to get seriously injured in a struggle like that. Your Lordships might imagine a kind of cage, as it were, where men struggle like wild beasts, we stand upon one another's shoulders. I myself have had 8 or 10 men on my shoulders and my head, and I have been hurt several times in a struggle for employment like that.'
>
> *Select Commons Committee on the Sweating System 1888*

TRADES UNIONS

By the 1880s workers in unskilled as well as skilled jobs were organising into trades unions in order to improve their wages and working conditions. Although the first trades unions of the 1860s were mostly for men, women in textile factories started forming unions in the 1870s, and the Women's Trade Union League was set up in 1874 to link women's unions on a national basis. In 1888, the 'Match Girls Strike' at Bryant and May was a tremendous victory, because unskilled women workers had taken strike action for the first time, and won their claim for higher wages and better conditions. In 1889 another very important victory was won by the dockers, again an unskilled union, who secured a minimum rate of pay and other improvements in their conditions of work.

In order to get higher wages, male trades unionists often argued that they had wives and children to support. Employers would therefore pay women less and keep them in the lowest-paid jobs. Some male unions adopted the 'middle-class' view that women shouldn't work at all, in order to campaign for a higher 'family wage' for themselves. This attitude was expressed at the 1877 TUC by Harry Broadhurst:

> 'It was their duty as men and husbands to use their utmost efforts to bring about a condition of things where their wives would be in their proper sphere at home instead of being dragged into competition for livelihood against the great and strong men of the world.'

Women trades unionists had a different point of view. They wanted the men's support to get a decent wage for women as well as men:

> 'The real point to be complained of is the low rate of payment earned by the women, and the way to prevent the employment of women in any trade they are unfit for, is for men to join in helping them to combine in order that they may receive the same wages for the same work.'
>
> **Clementina Black, 1887 TUC**

Men also got higher wages and the better-paid jobs because it was easier for them to belong to a union and take part in union activities. Women had home commitments, and women leaders found it much harder to organise their members:

> 'The single women often look upon their work as merely a temporary necessity . . . The married women find that home duties fill in such leisure time as they have when the day's work in the factory or workshop is over. Their estimate of their own position is a low one and they seem to think . . . that any display of independence on their part would oust them from the labour market entirely.'
>
> **Women's Trades Council, First Annual Report, 1890**

RESPECTABLE WORK – DOMESTIC SERVICE

The most common job for women in the 1880s and 90s was domestic service; about one in three unmarried women were servants. For men, it was the second most important occupation, after agriculture. The job varied from working in a large household with many servants, good food, and plenty of workmates, to being the sole servant, responsible for everything. Domestic service was not a job to be proud of and many girls pretended they did something else to their boyfriends, but it was considered respectable, especially for women, because it meant working inside the home under supervision. It was thought to be a good training for marriage too.

For men, service could mean a secure and regular income, leading to promotion and a relatively comfortable way of life eventually. A male butler might be married and live 'out'. By the end of the century male servants were increasingly hard to find (there were plenty of other jobs around for men) and therefore employers treated them with more respect. They became status symbols, and men employed as butlers and footmen to look impressive were given smart uniforms; women by contrast were supposed to be invisible and simply get on with the housework unnoticed.

Mrs Beeton, who wrote a famous book on household matters, suggested the following wages, in 1888:

General maid (housework)	£10–£16 a year
Cook	£16 a year
Valet (man's personal servant)	£35 a year
Footman . . . 5 foot 6 inches	£20–£22 a year
. . . up to 6 foot	£32–£40 a year

Mrs Beeton, *Book of Household Management*

RULES FOR SERVANTS

What made service different from other jobs was the control employers had over their employees. In this respect, women were more restricted than men.

' *"No Followers"*, meaning no boyfriends, was a common condition in advertisements for women servants. All "flirting" and "courting" had to be kept secret. This was because employers did not want their servants to get married and leave them, especially if they were good workers.

"Compulsory Uniform" Men usually wore dark suits or evening dress; women had to buy or make a cotton dress for the mornings, black wool with white cap and apron for the afternoons. Many

employers would give their girls a length of material for their Christmas present to make up their uniforms.

"*Instant Dismissal*" without a reference if you were found pregnant. Female servants were considered "easy prey" for the men of the house and were quite often seduced.

"*Be Invisible*" "If you are a housemaid be careful not only to do your work quietly but keep out of sight as much as possible. When meeting any ladies or gentlemen about the house, stand back or move aside for them to pass." (*Ladies' Magazine*)

"*Religion*" Tracts from the Bible like "Servants be obedient to them that are your masters" were often hung over a servant's bed. "No Irish need apply" was often written on adverts for servants, because people would not employ a Catholic. Servants had to go to church but sat at the back separately. Often they had to attend daily family prayers.'

Some ex-housemaids remember how they were treated:

'I got one job in a provost's house and while I was there I sprained my ankle and my foot was swollen up. The doctor said I should stop walking on it and rest for a fortnight. That did it. After three days her ladyship came and said, "I can't afford to have you fed and clothed and paid wages for doing nothing. You can have your notice."

'In service you usually had either the garret with all the lumber or the basement with stone floors and old furniture. There were all sorts of limitations. If you had curly hair you had to comb it straight back into a bun even at the age of fourteen. You had to wear long black dresses that fell over your shoes. They had two bathrooms in

" HMM! SOME CHRISTMAS PRESENT ~ TWO LENGTHS OF MATERIAL FOR A NEW UNIFORM. "

the house where I was, but we weren't allowed to use them. We had
to have our baths in the copper in the outhouse with another girl
holding the door in case the men came in. They seemed to think the
working class lived like pigs. I had to say "Yes Milady" and "No
Milady" whenever I spoke.'

Jessie Stephens, Bristol 1978

'I worked as a scullery maid in a home where there were two
mentally defective children. You got up at six and worked 'til you
went to bed. There was no free time, nowhere to sit down, not like in
the big houses in "Upstairs, Downstairs". I got half a day off on
Sunday when I walked four miles home to see my mother.'

Mrs Shaw, London 1978

One servant remembers having to iron *The Times* each day, and stitch the
pages together to keep it neat. Then she had to iron perfume into the pages
for the lady of the house. Sometimes, servants were tested by tricks such as
hiding coins under the carpet. If the coins were left there it showed that they
had skimped their work. If the coins were removed, the servant was considered dishonest!

THE GOVERNESS

For the middle classes, work was a very different matter. A man might go
into business, or for those with education and qualifications there was the
law, the church or medicine. There were very few jobs that middle-class
women could do, and they only worked if they had fallen on hard times and
had no-one to support them. Before the 1870s, becoming a governess was
about the only acceptable work. It meant a lonely life, living in someone
else's house but apart from the other servants. Pay was low (£20–£35 a
year on average, or sometimes only board and keep). One governess wrote
in 1884:

'An advertisement in *The Times* for a governess now attracts several
hundred offers, more than half offering to go for nothing. They
think, these good people, that we ought to teach their spoilt,
insolent children, play with them, mend their clothes for them, take
their insults and bear their tempers and even do a little housemaid's
work for a bare living and perhaps a cast-off dress sometimes. The
children know we come for nothing and they coolly tell us that if we
don't please them they'll soon get "Mamma to send you away."
"And if Mamma sends you away you'll starve Miss. You've got no
money you know." That's what the children say to us. They are not
children but cruel little heartless bullies who have already learnt
how to sit upon the poor.'

A children's nanny (1884)

The governess was often regarded as a social outcast:

> 'She is a bore to almost any gentleman, as a tabooed woman . . .
> she is a bore to most ladies by the same rule. The servants invariably
> detest her for she is dependent like themselves and yet, for all that,
> as much their superior in other respects as the family they both
> serve.'
>
> *The Quarterly Review*, 1881

TEACHING

Following the Education Act 1870 there was an increasing demand for
teachers, and teaching became one of the few alternative jobs for middle-
class girls. However, school-teaching meant contact with the poor, something of a new experience to many as this magazine article pointed out:

> 'We have no doubt many ladies would find the class of children they
> would be required to teach a great trial to them, as the habits and
> ideas of children of the lower classes would, in all probability, prove
> a considerable shock to the sensibilities of ladies who came into
> contact with them for the first time.'
>
> *The Quarterly Review*, 1877

More often, the job of teaching in a Board school attracted working-class girls, who could train from the age of thirteen as pupil-teachers and perhaps later go to college to qualify. Three out of four pupil-teachers were women, who were found to stick to the training course better than men: after all, this was still more attractive than many of the other jobs open to them.

Once qualified, however, male teachers were automatically paid more for the same job — £40 a year more in 1880. Because they were cheaper, School Boards were keen to employ women. Men teachers were more likely to teach older children in the few secondary schools. One reason given for restricting women to primary schools was that it was felt to be unwise for them to teach older boys as they might not be able to keep order:

> 'If only discipline can be secured, female influence is likely to be beneficial . . . but the employment of women to teach boys over ten years of age would scarcely be entertained at present.'
>
> Committee on the Supply of Teachers, 1880

Women were often dismissed if they married:

> 'In consequence of the great inconvenience and confusion which is periodically caused in the Board Schools by married female teachers, the Board of Managers considers it expedient that in future it be made a condition of appointment that all female teachers under the Board must resign on their marriage and further, this committee is of the opinion that by so doing, the welfare of the children will be forwarded.'
>
> Battersea School Managers, 1893

SHOPWORK

A further opportunity for women at this time was shopwork. Before the 1870s, most shops were family run, for example, the family grocer, selling goods that were packaged on the premises. Any staff employed were men who served an apprenticeship. By 1900, more and more goods were pre-packaged, and the first large stores employing many assistants were opening. Less skill was needed, so apprenticeship declined; the most important aspect of the job was to attract customers. Shop owners started to employ women, especially young and attractive ones, and shopwork gradually became largely women's work, a trend that has continued up to the present day. The job appealed to girls who wanted something a 'cut above' factory work. These were the attractions, according to one writer in 1891:

> 'The work is fairly agreeable, Sundays and evenings are one's own, this to many being an inestimable advantage, and then there is the pleasure of always being able to look nice and neat, also the charm of variety.'
>
> V. Karsland, *Women and their Work*

In fact shop assistants had much to complain about. One joke among factory workers was that 'counter jumpers', as they were nicknamed, were paid yearly as their wages were too small to divide by the week. Wages varied from the West End stores in London, who paid their girls £1 per week in the 1880s to local shops paying only 7/– or 8/– (35–40p). Hours varied too, West End stores closing early, while local shops kept their assistants to 11 or 12 o'clock at night. In 1889, one London draper was prosecuted for working two young boys ninety-four hours in one week; he was fined 3/6d (17½p).

One of the worst complaints was that, throughout this long day, assistants were never allowed to sit down, as this was considered a sign of inattentiveness. One London firm provided seats, but told their assistants: 'The young ladies had better not use them if they wish to retain their situations.'

There were often strict rules to follow. Whiteleys, a large London store, had nearly two hundred. Here are some of them:

Section 14: DISCIPLINE

144. Gossiping, loitering, standing close together, or making unnecessary noise, is Strictly Prohibited.

. . .

148. No one to enter or leave business by any other than the appointed doors under pain of dismissal.

. . .

151. No Assistant to be insolent to shopwalkers or buyers.
154. No young man to have his coat off in the shop while it is open.
155. No Assistant to stand on a chair.
156. No Toilet Business, Nail Cleaning & etc. to be done in the Shops or Showrooms.

Laws passed to regulate hours and conditions of work in shops were slow to take effect, in spite of the unions, and it was not until 1963 that shop workers won the same standards of safety and comfort as factory workers.

OFFICE WORK

Clerical work was expanding rapidly by the 1880s. As industry grew, so did banking, accounting, insurance and communications of all kinds, requiring a new workforce. At the same time shorthand was introduced and new machines were invented – the typewriter, telegraph and telephone.

These light machines were thought to be suitable for women to operate. The typewriter was reckoned to be rather like playing the piano – the knobs

"M'DEAR, IS THIS HAIRSTYLE MEANT TO STOP YOU HEARING MY VOICE OR THE CLATTER OF THE KEYS?"

are still called 'keys'. So office work offered a new kind of employment for respectable girls. Hours and conditions of work were relatively good. The attraction of women for employers was that they could pay them less; at the turn of the century, most male clerks earned over £2 a week, but most females about £1. A woman clerk confirms this:

> 'It requires you to have a good plain education to do our work. There is a head gentleman clerk over us . . . the firm likes lady clerks best: for they do the work as well as the gentlemen and are paid less.'
> Derek Hudson, *Munby, Man of Two Worlds*

Magazines offered advice on how to dress for the office:

> 'We would like to suggest that the large pads of hair that are worn sometimes completely covering the ears, must, to some extent, impede the hearing, which should be as keen as possible when taking notes.'
> *Oliver Magazine*

The first typewriter firms often hired out both the machine and the female operator − who was called a 'typewriter' for a while − to an office to do their typing. With shorthand, a woman could earn as much as 30/– (£1.50p) a week in the 1890s. Because of opportunities like these, the number of women clerical workers increased by 400% between 1861 and 1911.

The first clerical workers' union was formed in 1889, but in spite of the large number of women in offices, men and women had different rates of pay for the same work until the recent Equal Pay Act made this illegal.

90

MEDICINE – NURSING

Working in medicine only became respectable for women at the end of the century. Nurses had, up to this time, been regarded as low-class women who were unable to find any better means of earning a livelihood. After Florence Nightingale opened the first nurses training school at St Thomas's Hospital in London in 1860, nursing schools were gradually established throughout the country, offering 2–4 year courses and a nursing certificate. It became an occupation for ladies, and magazines advertised the attractions to their readers:

> 'It is pre-eminently women's work, so there is no competition from men, no thought of lowering the wages of male breadwinners, or facing black looks from students of the other sex. The chief attraction is the esteem in which attendance on the sick is held. This makes the work satisfactory in itself.'
>
> *The Young Lady Magazine*, 1893

It was also supposed to be a vocation:

> 'Nurses are supposed to take it up in a missionary spirit for the good of the community without regard to their comfort and health.'
>
> Bulley and Whitley, *Women's Work*, 1894

There were also warnings of the hardships:

> 'Nurses are liable to premature decline, rheumatic nervous suffering in old age . . . Attending patients of the opposite sex would prove a severe nervous test and could only be overcome by long steady and conscientious practice.'
>
> *Fraser's Magazine*, 1891

Mrs Shaw, a woman who worked as a nurse in the 1900s, describes what it was like:

> 'The other nurses were more upper class than me, and I had less education than them but I was more intelligent. The matrons and sisters were terrible – so catty. Everyone was in strict order – the person who came an hour before you went before you. I had bobbed hair and the matron said if she'd known that she wouldn't have taken me. She said "You look like the scrubbers" – those were the women who came in to clean the floor. We did twelve hours all night without a break and nothing to eat – I used to take cabbages from the garden. Sunday morning we got one sausage as a treat. We had to be in by ten and boys weren't allowed to say goodnight to you at the gate. You couldn't leave the building unless it was your evening off. If you had free time during the day you had to go to lectures.

> There was one doctor and he didn't speak to you until you were in the
> position of sister.'

In the 1890s, trainee nurses earned £12 a year rising to £50 a year for a
sister, including free board and lodging. The financial problem persisted for
nurses as few of them could find work after the age of forty, and there were
no pensions until the first insurance schemes were set up in the 1880s.

DOCTORS

The better paid and more highly qualified work of doctors was for a long
time open to men only, but in the 1870s the struggle for women to become
doctors began. Elizabeth Garrett Anderson qualified as the first English
woman doctor, and a few women now attended medical school regularly.
Dr Helena Wright, one of the first women to qualify before the First World
War, describes her experiences:

> 'We were all oddities to some extent. To be a medical student then
> you had to really want to do it. The Royal Free was the only hospital
> brave enough to take on women. We were the first women doctors
> any of the hospitals had had. They didn't know how to treat us. They

Women delivering coke during World War I

92

said, "How will they deal with the drunks on Saturday night?" when I was one of the doctors in charge of out-patients. They soon realised that there was no nonsense about it at all – no friction and atmosphere with the nurses as there was with young men. When the hospital got used to having women they found it was much better. The doctors could be friends with the sisters. Many women patients liked having women doctors too.'

Dr Wright worked in a military hospital in London for wounded soldiers during the First World War, with thirteen male doctors: 'I gave the men the choice of being able to refuse being operated on by a woman. Not a single patient objected. The hospital went on as normal and there was a very happy atmosphere.'

MODERN TRENDS

Over the last hundred years the division of work between women and men has basically continued to follow the pattern that developed in the late nineteenth century. Men have tended to work in heavy industry and skilled jobs; women have increasingly been concentrated in white collar and service jobs, replacing their previous role as domestic servants. Some jobs, (for example, being a secretary) were originally done by men. But when women moved in to this work the status of the job fell.

1975 – Women as a percentage of the total workforce	
Typists and secretaries	98.6%
Nurses	91.6%
Canteen assistants	96.8%
Cleaners	91.7%
Shop assistants	81%

However, the development of this trend has not been continuous throughout the last century. Changes in the economic circumstances of the country have caused major changes and reversals in men's and women's work at different times. During the First World War, for example, when men were needed to fight, women were encouraged to take over their jobs and to do traditionally 'masculine' work, like manufacturing arms and explosives.

Women were praised for doing jobs like delivering coal, where previously they would have been condemned. While doing these jobs under the same conditions as men, women had a hard struggle to get the same rates of pay, and were often forced to accept lower rates. After the war, when the men returned, women had to give up the jobs. A similar situation occurred again during the Second World War, 1939–45.

The Equal Pay and Sex Discrimination Acts of 1975 require that all jobs, with certain exceptions such as mining, should be open to both sexes for the same pay. So far the effects of these laws have been limited, for although women can and do now enter the professions and management, the top jobs are still dominated by men: only 8% of barristers, 4% of architects and 1% of chartered accountants are women. Two out of three women work in ten occupations which include office and shop work, teaching, nursing and clothing manufacture. In 1980 women's average earnings in Britain were three-quarters of men's. It is often said that women work for 'pin money' and extras and that their work is financially less important than men's. In fact, a recent report on family poverty found that most women have to work to make ends meet, even when they have working husbands, and many do not have working husbands. The report commented:

> **'In many cases the employment of married women represents the dividing line between poverty and adequate living standards.'**
> **Townsend Report, 1980**

Although women today have many more job opportunities, they still do not have equal opportunities with men. Just as a hundred years ago all sorts of excuses were found to keep the more highly skilled and better paid jobs for men, so today employers were found to believe that 'Women are better at dull, repetitive jobs' (*Office of Population Survey*, 1975).

While working lives in Britain have changed in many ways over the last century, the evidence suggests that in many respects work prospects are still very different for men and women.

QUESTIONS

A hundred years ago p. 67:

1. Why do you think 'there was no thought of a career' for working-class people, according to Emily Bishop? How far are things different today?

2. Compare the typical working life of men and women as outlined on page 68. What were the major factors that made them different? How has the pattern changed today?

In the country p. 69 and 'Unladylike' p. 71:

3. How does the evidence indicate that men's work and women's work were both hard, but in different ways?

4. Why were fewer women employed in agricultural labouring by the end

of the nineteenth century, according to the evidence here? What do the government reports of 1864 and 1867 indicate about attitudes to women at that time?

Heavy work p. 72;

5.   Compare the description of women saltworkers by Brian Didsbury with the inspector's report. Do you think there was any justification for his fears about immorality? What do you think the motives behind his evidence might have been?

Wearing the trousers p. 73:

6.   Why do you think people disapproved of women wearing trousers, even for dirty work? It has only recently become acceptable for women to wear trousers for work. In which jobs would it still not be accepted?

7.   What do the extracts from Munby and Strachey tell us about the attitudes of women in heavy jobs towards their work? Do you think those jobs were fit for women to do? Were they fit for men to do?

Dangerous jobs p. 76:

8.   From the two extracts, what were the dangers in mining and iron making at this time? Would you expect these jobs to be any less dangerous now? What jobs would you expect to be most dangerous in Britain today?

9.   Try to find out the figures for industrial accidents today. Do you think working conditions have become safer?

Factory work p. 77:

10.   Do you think there was, or is, any truth in the reasons given by employers for giving women and men different kinds of work? What jobs would you expect to find women and men doing in factories today?

11.   George Sturt suggests that skilled labour was more satisfying a hundred years ago than today. Why?

Rules and regulations p. 79:

12.   Why were employers like Courtaulds able to govern their workers' lives more than they could today? Why did they have greater control over the women than the men?

The sweated trades p. 80:

13.   Why do you think wages and conditions for women were worse for home workers? Is this the case today?

14.   According to the extract on page 82, why was dock work humiliating? In what ways can work or unemployment be humiliating today?

Trades unions p. 82:

15.   Whose argument do you agree with; Harry Broadhurst's or

Clementina Black's? Why did men and women trades unionists have opposing points of view?

16. According to the Women's Trades Council, why were there more men than women trades unionists? Does the same situation apply today?

Respectable work p. 84:

17. Based on the interviews and rules quoted, what do you think were the worst aspects of working in service, and what were the advantages?

The governess p. 86 and Teaching p. 87:

18. From the evidence on page 88, how did job opportunities in teaching differ for men and women? How was this justified? Do teachers have the same opportunities today?

Shopwork p. 88 and Office work p. 89:

19. According to the extracts and facts given, what were the attractions of working in shops and offices for men and for women? Do they do the same kinds of work in shops and offices today?

Medicine p. 91:

20. According to the writers on page 91, why was nursing suitable for women? According to Helena Wright, why did people think that for women to work as doctors presented problems? Do you think we now accept men and women equally as both nurses and doctors?

Modern trends p. 93:

21. Why do you think, in spite of recent legislation for equal opportunities, women do not earn as much as men, nor get the same jobs? Do you think this will change in the future?

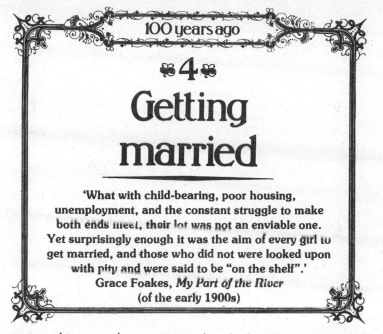

❧4❧
Getting married

'What with child-bearing, poor housing,
unemployment, and the constant struggle to make
both ends meet, their lot was not an enviable one.
Yet surprisingly enough it was the aim of every girl to
get married, and those who did not were looked upon
with pity and were said to be "on the shelf".'
Grace Foakes, *My Part of the River*
(of the early 1900s)

For most working people, marriage a hundred years ago meant a hard struggle financially. It was very much a partnership in which husband and wife each had their separate roles. The man worked as hard as he could to earn money while the woman managed the finances (adding to them if she could by working), brought up the children, and ran the home single-handed. But in spite of economic hardship, most young people wanted to find a partner and set up a home, as they do today.

KEEPING COMPANY

For working people, the usual place to meet someone was on the local 'monkey parade' as it was called. This is what it was like in Bolton in the 1880s:

'The procedure was to parade the principal streets on Saturday and Sunday evenings, each sex in groups or couples until some adventurous male would make the first advance with some fatuous remark such as "Can I see you home, Miss". If the girls responded this constituted a sort of introduction. The same groups would meet for several weeks and chat together before ultimately pairing off. Sometimes it all ended with nothing definite, and the groups began to parade again. But in many cases couples who met in this way

97

became engaged and later were happily married. It was most inno-
cent and pleasant and in a sense was the working girls' equivalent of
the London season.'

Hannah Mitchell, The Hard Way Up

Going steady with someone was called 'walking out' or 'keeping
company' and in fact, since there was little privacy at home, going walking
was often the only way to be alone:

'Dancing rooms being often taboo, and visits to each other's
crowded kitchens impossible, youthful couples walked the streets or
stood in dark doorways, often to be duly remarked and reported on.'

Robert Roberts, The Classic Slum

Parents were strict about going out, especially with their daughters:

'Teenagers, especially girls, were kept on a very tight reign. Father
fixed the number of evenings on which they could go out and
required to know precisely where and with whom they had spent
their leisure. He set, too, the exact hour of their return; few dared
break the rule. One neighbour's daughter, a girl of nineteen, was
beaten for coming home ten minutes late after choir practice.'

Robert Roberts, The Classic Slum

One woman remembers coming home with her boyfriend:

'My mother came to the corner of the street and said "Come on, get
yourself in. He's no better than he ought to be to keep you out after
nine o'clock." Nine o'clock! And when I was going to be married and
how old was I, twenty-three, I came in, opened the door, and he was
with me and my mother shouted down the stairs, "What time do you
call this coming in?" You know, very strict.'

Elizabeth Roberts, 'Working Class Women in the North West'

A single girl who got pregnant brought disgrace to her family:

'If a single girl had a baby she lowered not only the social standing of
her family, but in some degree that of all her relatives.'

Robert Roberts, A Ragged Schooling

If this happened, many parents insisted that the boy married the girl. One
man described what his father's reaction would have been:

'There wouldn't have been no flying their kites and then changing
their minds. They'd have had to marry the girl, if she'd been good
enough to do that with she'd have been good enough to marry and
that would have been Dad's lot.'

Elizabeth Roberts, 'Working Class Women in the North West'

GETTING ENGAGED

Sex before marriage was not only disapproved of — it was very risky as contraceptives were not yet available to working-class people. Because there was less sexual freedom than today, sometimes kissing and petting only went on once a couple were engaged. The boy would ask the girl's father for permission to get engaged, which was often quite an ordeal:

> 'I blurted out "Have you any objection to Daisy and I getting married?" Her father said, "This is a bit sudden." I then corrected myself and said, "I mean engaged." Her father said he'd no objection as long as we knew what it meant and saved for a good start.'
>
> George Noakes, *To be a Farmer's Boy*

Long engagements of three or four years while a couple saved up, were quite common. The average age for getting married was about twenty-five for girls and twenty-seven for boys. Today it's twenty-three for girls and twenty-five for boys. A woman who was courting in the 1900s said: 'I wouldn't get married until we had saved up enough to make a start. We used to buy two pennyworth of sweets and go for long walks to save money.'

Lack of money often made marriage out of the question for a long time. Grace Foakes described how she felt when she got the unexpected offer of a house from a relative:

> 'Though we'd been courting there had never been any talk of marriage because it had seemed impossible without years of saving first. Alas for romance, my mind was so busy on mental arithmetic that I hardly appreciated that this was a proposal.'
>
> Grace Foakes, *My Part of the River*

On the other hand, among the very poor, lack of comfort at home may have encouraged early marriage just to get away:

> 'At the East End it is the rule for every boy of 15 or 16 to be engaged to a girl with whom he is "keeping company" as it is termed. Walking out with a girl among the working classes absolutely implies engagement. I pass down the murky alley and on each doorstep I see a boy and girl of comparatively tender years locked in each others arms or hand clasped in hand. They are all of them waiting for the first possibility of swarming out from the parent hive. No doubt at home they are crowded and uncomfortable, they have no privacy; the prospect of a room to themselves presents great attractions. So as soon as the boy is earning 12 or 15 shillings [60–75p] the girl 8 or 10 [40–50p] marriage seems practicable.'
>
> *Eastward Ho Magazine*, 1885

WEDDINGS

For most people, a wedding was not an elaborate occasion – much more fuss was made over funerals. People saved all their lives for a good burial, but had little to spend on a wedding. This was the normal custom in Middlesborough:

> 'On the wedding day the parents of the bride do not generally go to the church; sometimes the mother remains at home to superintend the cooking of the wedding feast; sometimes she is simply too busy to get out, and the wedding is merely an incident in the daily work. The young man and young woman go off together to church with another man and girl who fulfil the functions of groomsman and bridesmaid respectively. They go on foot, or, if they can afford it, in a four-wheel cab. After the wedding is over they go back to their own house, and either have a day off and enjoy themselves or else the man goes straight back to his work and the wife to her new home.'
>
> Lady Florence Bell, *At the Works*

Hannah Mitchell, a working-class woman who later became a suffragette, married in Oldham in 1895. In her autobiography she described her

Wedding group (1907)

wedding, which was more elaborate than was usual at that time for people in her class. She was earning 18/– (90p) a week as a shop assistant, her fiancé 25/– (£1.25p):

'The wedding was a very simple one, although my three brides-maids were a novelty for working-class folk in those days. Although my sister and I were very proud of the wedding breakfast we prepared, we only regarded it as a very modest spread. We had a boiled ham, a big piece of roast beef, pickles, fruit pies, sponge cakes, fruit cakes, jellies and trifles, tea and coffee with cream. My brother-in-law provided wine, beer and cigars. The friends and relatives present were generous with their gifts of linen, china and bedding for our future home.

When I rose early on my wedding day I found that every neighbour had risen earlier still, cleaned her windows, and whitened the flags [paving stones] both back and front, thus giving the whole street a festive appearance on that glorious September morning. The memory is clearer than any other I retain of my wedding day.

There were no speeches or toast drinking at the wedding break-fast; but plenty of happy talk. Later we all went for a walk in the local park, returning for an ample tea. We left early to return to Bolton and to work next morning, the wedding having been arranged to take place on the weekly half-holiday. But for the pioneers who had won for shop workers this weekly respite, we should have had to be married on a Sunday as many working folk were in those days.'

Hannah Mitchell, *The Hard Way Up*

Living together is often assumed to be a modern idea, but among the very poor in cities many couples didn't bother with a wedding at all:

'Marriage as an institution is not fashionable in these districts. Yet as long as cohabitation is possible, that is to say so long as neither the hospital, the prison nor the churchyard effects a separation, the couples are fairly faithful and look upon themselves as man and wife with the usual marital obligations. If you ask the couples who live happily why they don't get married some will tell you frankly that they never gave it a thought, others that it is a lot of trouble and they haven't got the time.'

George Sims, *How the Poor Live*, 1883

MIDDLE-CLASS COURTSHIP – CHAPERONES

Working couples during their courting and engagement enjoyed a fairly equal relationship, saving up together. For the middle and upper classes it was quite different. Girls had a very sheltered and restricted

101

upbringing and were never allowed to be alone with a boy without a chaperone until they were actually engaged. This meant that even getting to know someone well enough to want to get engaged was sometimes quite difficult! When a girl from a wealthy family reached about seventeen she had a 'coming out' dance. This was a big occasion when she made her entry into adult social life.

> 'As I came nearer this romantic moment, people enquired of my mother "Is your daughter out yet?" Which meant, could she go to adult parties or could she not. Everything was routine ridden and completely cut and dried. If you weren't out you were in. This meant schoolroom supper with milk and a bun. To be out meant having young men, so far not encouraged but very much wanted . . . The white dress was made and kept shrouded in a sheet in the spare room. As it was to be a January dance, it was trimmed with fluffy white swansdown and artificial lilies-of-the-valley which were thought to be girlish.'
>
> Ursula Bloom, *Requesting the Pleasure*

There were strict rules about how to behave:

> 'It was the world's dullest dance but I adored it. I was permitted only two dances with the same young man lest people talked. I surmised that people seemed to talk very easily and about nothing. I managed to get in three dances however, with a gawky young man called Nigel who worked at the brewery and was "something of a

" YOU REALISE, OF COURSE, WHAT SHARING AN UMBRELLA IMPLIES ? "

one". "But dear, be careful. Only choose professional young men, not men in trade," said my chaperone, warning me of the dire consequences of such misbehaviour.'

Ursula Bloom, Requesting the Pleasure

A girl had both to behave herself and also to mix only with boys who would make suitable husbands. That's why the supervision of the chaperone was so important. A good chaperone was described like this in the 1880s:

'A lady possessing a large circle of acquaintances who is popular as well as good natured . . . throughout the whole evening introducing the young lady in her care to those ladies in her acquaintance who are most in the habit of giving entertainments and by introducing any gentlemen to her whom she thinks would be likely to ask her to dance.'

Manners and Rules of Good Society

PROBLEM PAGES

Many middle-class girls wrote to magazines like *Girls' Own* for advice on how to behave. Here are some of the replies, written in 1895:

'Dear Sack: How comes it that you sometimes walk with a gentleman, if not engaged to him? If your intended husband, you may of course, walk under one umbrella; but otherwise you had better keep your own to yourself.'

'Dear Tootsie: Go by all means to see your betrothed husband, but take your sister with you.'

'Dear Ta-ra-ra: It surprises me to find that a girl sufficiently educated to write and spell well should be so deplorably ignorant of the common rules of society to think she may go out alone with a young man in his canoe. And furthermore, one whom she "only knows slightly".'

The pressure to find a husband for middle-class girls was strong because they were not expected to work for a living, and so had to find a man to support them. Their parents would be most anxious to get them off their hands so that they did not have to feed and clothe them for ever. And it looked bad, socially, to have daughters who had failed to marry.

While there might have been more freedom for young men from the same background, they had the job of persuading the girl's father not only of their good character but of their ability to provide financially for her. If his prospects weren't good, a man didn't stand much of a chance, as one young man described:

Three sisters being presented at court at their 'coming out' (1901)

'An ever memorable day in my life. I went over to the vicarage at ten o'clock and had a long talk with him on the lawn about my attachment to Daisy. Ways, means and prospects. I was frightfully nervous. "I am attached to one of your daughters," I said.

'Mr Thomas said I had done quite right in coming to him. He said also a great many complimentary things about my "honourable high-minded conduct", asked what my prospects were and shook his head over them. He could not allow an engagement under the circumstances, he said, and I must not destroy his daughter's peace of mind by speaking to her or showing her in any way that I was attached to her.'

The Reverend Kilvert, Kilvert's Diary

MARRIAGE – A PARTNERSHIP

Many people, in describing working-class marriage at the end of the last century, have emphasised the hard struggle by both partners against poverty:

> 'For eight months my husband tramped from early morning till late at night looking for work, and during all that time he did small jobs that brought in £3 in all. I had tried to help the situation by first going out to work and then by doing washing at home. I turned my hand to anything that would honestly bring in money.'
>
> Mrs Layton, 'Memories of Seventy Years', in Margaret Llewelyn Davies (ed) *Life As We Have Known It*

Compared to better-off women, working-class women aged quickly once they were married:

> 'One's heart aches at seeing a girl of twenty-four or twenty-five, when she ought to be at her best, most joyous, most hopeful – at the age when the well-to-do girl, in these days apt to marry later, is often still leading a life of amused irresponsibility and enjoyment – already appearing dulled, discouraged, her form almost shapeless, her looks gone.'
>
> Lady Florence Bell, *At the Works*

Of course, men aged too under the pressure of very hard work. The most difficult years were when there were a number of young children to bring up:

> 'The time when existence seems to press most hardly is during the first twelve or fourteen years after marriage, when there is usually a family of young children, who have to be provided for and who cannot earn; and the wife is constantly, before and after every birth, in a condition in which she cannot fulfil her duties with efficiency. It is not until later that the husband's wages are supplemented by odds and ends of work on the part of the wife, when she has a daughter old enough to leave in charge of the house, and also by earnings of one kind or another from sons and daughters employed in other callings.'
>
> Lady Florence Bell, *At the Works*

What made a good husband or a good wife? Here are some comments made by men and women who remember their parents' marriages at the turn of the century.

<table>
<tr><td>A GOOD HUSBAND</td></tr>
<tr><td>'He never left her short on the housekeeping money.'
'He was very handy when he was at home.'
'He was very good with the children.'
'He didn't spend a lot on drink and he didn't smoke – he gave her practically everything he brought home.'</td></tr>
<tr><td>A GOOD WIFE</td></tr>
<tr><td>'She was the chancellor of the exchequer. She schemed and provided so that we didn't go without.'
'She never complained and she never had a day off in her life.'
'She kept the place spotless, and with six kids that wasn't easy.'
'She did any odd jobs she could get to try and help out with the money.'</td></tr>
</table>

UPS AND DOWNS

It's hard to find out what people really thought about their marriages – they were, and are, often reluctant to write or talk about their feelings.

Maud Pember Reeves carried out a survey among young wives in Lambeth, London in the 1900s. This is what she found:

> 'They spoke well of their husbands when they spoke of them at all, but it is the children chiefly who filled their lives. The woman who said "My young man's that good ter me I feel as if somethink nice 'ad 'appened every time 'e comes in," was obviously speaking the simple truth, and she was more articulate than most of the others whose " 'E's all right," might mean as much. Another woman introduced the subject as follows. " 'E's a good 'usbin. 'E ain't never kep' back me twenty-three bob, but 'e's that spiteful Satterday nights I 'as ter keep the children from 'im." "And what do you do?" asked the interested visitor. "Oh me? That's all right. I'm cooking 'is supper," she explained, as though to a child.'

> Maud Pember Reeves, *Round About a Pound a Week*

The young Lambeth wives referred to their husbands as 'my young man'. In Salford, near Manchester, they called them 'my boss' or 'my master'. It seems that in the North the man was traditionally the dominant partner, but according to this extract, not always the boss:

106

'After excessive drinking, food was the greatest source of local friction. A boozed-up husband coming in late would frequently complain about a meal being kept warm for him, or would push it away untouched. This habit women in the shop frequently bemoaned. "What can you do? Jack's that funny with his food. You can't please him." If the dinner was rejected most wives prepared an alternative dish, in an effort to suit the great one's palate. Others wept as he stamped off to bed, the children dodging in his path. Not every woman though, accepted the mighty male with subservience and tears. Bolder wives boasted at the counter of presenting the drunken late-comer with a burnt offering. One lady as soon as her "boss" turned down his meal called in a hungry dog from next door to polish it off on the spot. Mrs Huntley, who stood six feet and weighed fifteen stone, merely inverted a plate of hash over her spouse's head. I don't recall any of these husbands getting ham and pickle afterwards.'

Robert Roberts, *A Ragged Schooling*

FOR BETTER OR WORSE

For all but the very rich, marriage was for life. Divorce was simply out of the question on financial grounds alone. It cost about £150 for the court case and the full expense, with travelling and time off work could amount to £500. Legally, it was also very hard indeed to get a divorce — the law discouraged it, and few lawyers would give advice or deal with the case. Divorce was more difficult for women to obtain than men. A man could divorce his wife for adultery alone. A woman had to prove adultery plus some other grounds like cruelty. For working-class people it was usually economically impossible to survive as a divorced person, especially for

" BURNT OFFERING "

107

women. A wife could not support herself and her children alone; a man could not work and bring up his children on his own.

Even more important, the very idea of divorce was socially unacceptable. Divorced people were shunned and their children were believed to inherit 'bad blood'. Most people believed that it was right to put up with even a very bad marriage. Religion still had a strong influence on standards of morality, and marriage was traditionally a Christian institution, upheld by the Church. Even for the non-Churchgoing majority of the working classes, loyalty to one's marriage partner was regarded as right morally. This extract describes conditions in the East End of London:

'Although this was a poor working-class community, people had a great sense of values regarding moral behaviour. Each woman kept to her own man and would not have dreamed of doing otherwise. Sometimes the men were very cruel to their women, especially when in drink. I have heard many a woman screaming and shouting as a drunken man gave her a good hiding. The following day she would emerge with black eyes and a swollen face, yet would not utter a word against her husband – and woe betide anyone who did! Not a word would she have against him.'

Grace Foakes, *My Part of the River*

A South London couple (1900s)

" FOR BETTER OR WORSE "

This writer describes attitudes towards a separated woman:

'We had our outcasts also, a couple who were "living in sin". Our standards of sexual morality were high – though I'm not sure about the reasons behind it. In this case the woman had run away with the man, leaving her husband, and I once heard the comment: "We have to put up wi' our men, why shouldn't she put up wi' hers?" – a point of view with which the other women heartily agreed.'

Jane Walsh, *Not Like That*

This is a letter from the problem pages of a magazine in 1915:

'*Q*: I wonder if you will think me very wicked when I tell you that though I am a married woman, I do not love my husband and am not living with him? We married too young – I was eighteen and he twenty – and I soon discovered that he was not the man for me. Soon after I met the one man for me and though we have never been sweethearts, yet we have confessed our love . . . Is it my duty to live with a man I do not love when all my heart belongs to another? Do you think I am acting wickedly and ought I to go back to the man I married? – *Hester*

A: Not wicked Hester, but foolish and weak, dear. We cannot break away from sacred promises. When you took that man for your husband you undertook certain duties, that you are morally bound to fulfil – to help him, to comfort him, to cherish him, to make a home for him, to lead him towards a better land. Your married life has disappointed you. Well, often things we buy turn out quite different from what we hope they will be but we cannot cast them away and have our money back . . . Return to your husband, bury the love that can be nothing to you, and determine if you care for him as a wife should, to do your duty.'

Home Companion Magazine

By the 1880s a wife or husband could get a legal separation on grounds of cruelty or regular drunkenness, and wives could apply for a maintenance grant, but it was still very hard to leave, as Mrs Shaw, a midwife, explained:

> 'I once delivered someone of her thirteenth child – she was actually a battered wife. I said, "Why don't you leave him?" She said she'd got a separation after the sixth child but she'd come back because what else could she do? I had asked the question in my superior ignorance. For where could she go? There was no social security and no homes to go to.'

At the beginning of this century the Women's Co-operative Guild campaigned for easier divorce laws. They stressed in particular how much harder a bad marriage was for working-class people. The following is an extract from their report, which made a case for changing the law:

> 'It is far from right that the poor should have to suffer without remedy because it's expensive, a hateful companionship, while the rich, to whom such a companionship is not nearly so odious or galling as to poor people, in their small houses, can afford to pay for freedom. The law, if anything, should be made easier for the poor than the wealthy, seeing that in the majority of cases they are unable to even have separate bedrooms. Where the husband and wife cannot live happily together it is no real marriage. It is a fraud without love. If both are agreeable it is a sin to compel them for the sake of appearing man and wife to live in the same house when they are divided in reality.'

However, there was no reform of the divorce laws until the 1950s, and only recently has there ceased to be such a strong social stigma attached to being divorced.

MIDDLE-CLASS MARRIAGE

> 'With grace to bear even wrath and peevishness, she must learn and adopt his taste, study his disposition, and submit in short to all his desires with all that grateful compliance which in a wife is the surest sign of a sound understanding.'

Woman as She Is and Should Be, 1879

Among the wealthier classes, marriage was less of an equal partnership because women never worked for money and were therefore totally dependent on their husbands. Although they ran the home, they had the help of servants, which made the woman's contribution to the family's survival less vital too. Socially, they were supposed to submit to their husband's superiority, and there was plenty of advice on how to do this:

> 'A wife's duty is the promotion of the happiness of others . . . to make sacrifices that *his* enjoyment may be enhanced.'
>
> Mrs Beeton, *Book of Household Management*

> 'A married woman wanting [lacking] conversation might become weary, stale, flat and unprofitable in the estimation of her husband and finally might drive him from the home by the leaden weight of her uncompanionable society . . . Not conversation about books if her husband happens to be a fox hunter, nor conversations about fox hunting if he likes books, but exactly that kind of conversation which is best adapted to his tastes and habits.'
>
> Mrs Ellis, *Women of England*

The writer, Somerset Maugham, described one husband's attitude in one of his novels:

> 'You laugh my boy, you can't imagine marrying beneath you. You want a wife who's an intellectual equal. Your head is crammed full of ideas of comradeship. Stuff and nonsense my boy! A man doesn't want to talk politics to his wife and what do you think I care for Betty's views on differential calculus? A man wants a wife who can cook his dinner and look after his children. I've tried both and I know. I make a point of the children going to Sunday school and I like Betty to go to church. I think women ought to be religious. I don't believe myself, but I like women and children to.'
>
> Somerset Maugham, *Of Human Bondage*

" NOT CONVERSATION ABOUT BOOKS IF HE HAPPENS TO BE A FOX-HUNTER "

An Islington couple (1890s)

Many women were beginning to rebel against the restricted life that middle-class marriage offered at the end of the century. Because it was almost impossible to conform to the accepted idea of marriage and at the same time do some independent, useful work, many women were forced to choose between the two. Florence Nightingale, for example, who never married, expressed the frustrations of women's lives:

> 'Why have women passion, intellect, moral activity – these three and a place in society where no one of these three can be exercised? Widowhood, ill health or want of bread – these three explanations or excuses alone are supposed to justify a woman taking up an occupation . . .
>
> So many hours are spent every day in passively doing what conventional life tells us when we would gladly be at work . . . we can never pursue any object for a single two hours, for we can never command any regular leisure or solitude; and in social and domestic life one is bound, under pain of being thought sulky, to make a remark every two minutes.'
>
> Florence Nightingale, *Cassandra*, in Ray Strachey, *The Cause*

THE DOUBLE STANDARD

When it came to being sexually faithful in marriage, there was one law for men, another for women. If a man was unfaithful it was considered natural and excusable; if a woman was, it was unforgivable. This double standard was practised mostly among the upper and middle classes. Men had time, money and the opportunity to meet women, and prostitution flourished in the large cities where poor women could earn a living by meeting this demand. While single working men or those working away from home and in the army and navy may have used prostitutes, it was much more common among the wealthy.

In the 1870s the Contagious Diseases Acts were passed, requiring women living in certain towns where servicemen were stationed to be medically examined for venereal disease, under arrest if necessary, if they were suspected of being prostitutes. Josephine Butler, a woman from a wealthy family, led a national campaign against these laws. She travelled the country to gain support from working men and women and presented her arguments to the all-male government committee — no small feat at that time for a young woman. She pointed very clearly to the double standard that existed:

> 'A moral lapse in a woman is spoken of as an immensely worse thing than in a man, there is no comparison to be formed between them. There are certain expressions . . . plainly revealing the double standard that society has accepted. One of these is "he is only sowing his wild oats" . . . we never hear it carelessly or complacently

" WELL MR. FENWICK-SYMES! NOW YOU'VE 'AD YOUR IRREGULAR
INDULGENCE OF A NATURAL IMPULSE, HOW ABOUT MY MATTER OF GAIN?"

asserted of a young woman that she is only "sowing her wild oats". All legislation up to now has been directed against one sex only. We insist that it should be directed against both sexes and wherever it has been directed against the poor only we insist, and the working men insist, that it should also apply to the rich.'

The committee argued back:

'There is no comparison to be made between prostitutes and the men who consort with them. With one sex the offence is committed as a matter of gain, with the other it is an irregular indulgence of a natural impulse.'

Glen Petrie, *A Singular Iniquity*

As a result of the campaign, which was supported by many working men and also by prostitutes themselves, the Acts were abolished in 1886; but attitudes like those held by the committee did not change as quickly.

THE LAW AND MARRIAGE ABOUT 100 YEARS AGO

A husband could lock up his wife	until 1891
A husband could beat his wife	until 1879
A husband owned all his wife's earnings	until 1870
A husband owned all his wife's belongings, clothes, money	until 1882
A husband owned the home and joint possessions	until 1920

Yet in the 1870s one famous lawyer said: 'For her protection and benefit, so great a favourite is the female sex in the laws of England.'

And in 1870 a leading judge said: 'Wives are sufficiently protected, and why should they be allowed to have money in their pockets to deal with as they think fit I cannot understand.'

During the nineteenth century, the law had enforced women's financial dependence on their husbands, which made it difficult for them to have any real independence. The Married Women's Property Acts passed in 1870 and 1882 were very important steps in giving wives some freedom to run their own lives by giving them the right to keep their own earnings. By then, middle-class women had been campaigning against the marriage laws for some time. For example, in the 1850s Caroline Norton made headline news by winning the right for herself as a divorced woman to have custody of her young children. (Before this, the stigma of divorce had meant that a divorced woman, but not a divorced man, was considered unfit to bring up her own children.) In 1873, this new right for women was extended to include custody of children up to sixteen years of age.

As more and more women like Josephine Butler and Florence Nightingale began to fight for their rights, so married women gradually became less restricted to the home and more involved in things outside. In the 1870s, married women won the right to become factory inspectors, church wardens, workhouse governors, members of school boards and parish councillors. In the 1880s they won the right to vote in local elections and many were now actively campaigning for the right to the national vote.

STAYING SINGLE

'Without the hope of marriage she could be a thing broken, a fragment of humanity created for use, but never to be used.'

Anthony Trollope (late nineteenth century writer)

In the 1880s there were about half a million more women than men in Britain and by 1900 there were almost a million more. There were several reasons for this. More girls than boys survived childhood illnesses; fewer women than men died from accidents and injuries at work; more single men emigrated to other parts of the British Empire; many died fighting in the Boer War of the 1890s.

Working women who didn't marry often worked as servants, or stayed living with their families. If they set up home on their own, they would be regarded as odd. Robert Roberts described the attitude towards 'old maids' in Salford:

'We had those houses too where one or more "old maids". lived together without a man. They usually kept their windows, doorsteps and pavement scrupulously clean and invariably became the butts of some local housewives who sneered about the "old faggots" with nothing better to do. Spinsters deprived of male protection suffered constantly from the tricks of children trading on parental indulgence, and their lives could be made a misery. Many single women, middle-aged and elderly, through the mere fact of being single had much to put up with from the taunts of youth and the amused contempt of some married neighbours – a sort of cruelty that would not be tolerated today.'

Robert Roberts, *A Ragged Schooling*

115

Many women didn't marry because they were looking after their father or mother, often with brothers and sisters to support too, and felt they could not leave them. A Northumberland woman explains:

> 'Many times I was asked by my young man to marry him but I always felt I could not leave my family. Mother was gone and how could I leave my father and my brothers and sisters who looked to me and relied on me to provide for them?'

A single man was usually in a better position. He could earn enough to live independently and would not be expected to stay with his family. He could easily find somewhere to live as a lodger where he would get his meals cooked, his washing done, and be welcome for his financial contribution to the family.

Among the better off, too, single life was more difficult for women, because before the 1880s there were few jobs open to them – becoming a governess or a teacher, perhaps. A man in the same position could much more easily follow a career, earning enough to support himself and enjoy the pleasures of an independent social life.

Some men and women did not marry because their strongest feelings were towards their own sex but we have no evidence about this. Lesbianism was never mentioned – the very idea was impossible for people to confront in the nineteenth century. No one admitted that it existed – so much so that it was not even illegal. Homosexuality between men was illegal and there were severe penalties for it up to 1969.

One solution to the problem of 'surplus' women was to encourage them to emigrate to the colonies, Canada and Australia, or to America. There were schemes organised for sending boat loads of single women to these places. According to *Punch* magazine, the results were successful:

> 'All our difficulties arise from a superabundance of females. The only remedy for this is to pack up bag and baggage and send them away. Out of the female immigrants who recently arrived at Melbourne by the William Stewart, eight were married within 24 hours after their landing.'

MODERN MARRIAGE

Because of important social changes, marriage for both men and women has now changed. Widely available contraception has made an enormous difference to the lives of married women, which used to consist largely of pregnancies, childbirths and childrearing. With the use of labour-saving equipment, housework and cooking also take less time and it has now become acceptable for women of all classes to work outside the home, earn their own money, and achieve greater economic independence.

116

Married men's lives have changed too, as the average basic working week has been reduced from 55–60 hours to 35–40. Many more husbands have time to spend with their wives and children.

Young married couples today have more opportunity to share the chores and to help each other, instead of having such clearly divided responsibilities. They are more likely to move away from their parents and to be less dependent on their advice and habits. With fewer children to cope with, there is more time to be in each other's company and to enjoy some leisure together, rather than thinking only of where the next meal is coming from.

Marriage today is not necessarily for life. Divorce is legally and financially much easier, and roughly one in four marriages in Britain now ends in divorce. It has become more socially acceptable too as the religious and moral attitudes of the nineteenth century have gradually changed over the past hundred years, and particularly since the Second World War.

However, marriage is still far from being equal for men and women in the eyes of the law. For example:

TAX A wife's earnings are treated as part of her husband's when it comes to paying tax unless they especially ask to be taxed separately. If a wife is owed a tax rebate it is automatically sent to her husband unless *he* asks for it to be sent to her. Married men get a special tax allowance but married women don't.

BENEFITS A wife is not entitled to claim Supplementary Benefit from the State, as a single woman can. Her husband is supposed to support her, and if a single woman is living with a man she can't claim, for the same reason.

Financially there are inequalities too. Only one in twenty wives earns more than her husband. One recent study showed that three-quarters of husbands did not tell their wives what they earned. According to the Marriage Guidance Council, most arguments, including violent rows, are to do with money.

Still, in spite of much talk about the 'breakdown of marriage', most people today do get married rather than stay single. Recent surveys show that three out of four women and one out of two men are married by the time they are 25. By 30 only one in ten women and one in five men are unmarried. Of those who get divorced, the majority eventually remarry. Marriage seems to be no less popular than it was a hundred years ago.

QUESTIONS
Keeping company p. 97:

1. How far do you think customs have changed since the 'monkey parade', described by Hannah Mitchell on page 97? Who makes the first move today?

2. Judging from these quotations and interviews, how much control did parents have over young people's behaviour? Was it the same for girls and boys? Do you think things are the same today?

Getting engaged p. 99:

3. How did money affect young people's plans for marriage or living together a hundred years ago? Have things changed in this respect?

Weddings p. 100:

4. Compare Hannah Mitchell's wedding, and the photograph of a wedding, with what happens today.

Middle-class courtship p. 101:

5. In what ways did middle-class girls and women have to meet stricter standards of behaviour than the working classes? Are there class differences in courtship today?

6. What were the difficulties in courtship for middle-class boys and men? How far are boys still expected to be able to 'provide' for a girl today if they want to marry her?

Marriage p. 105:

7. According to these extracts, in what ways was married life a struggle for working-class people? Is it just as hard today?

8. In your opinion, would it be the same qualities as those quoted on page 106 which make a good husband and a good wife today, or would you look for other qualities? Would they be different for a man and for a woman, as they are here?

Ups and downs p. 106:

9. What do these two extracts illustrate about the attitudes of husbands and wives at that time?

For better or worse p. 107:

10. What was the basis for the sense of loyalty described by Grace Foakes on page 108 and Jane Walsh on page 109? Do such attitudes still exist today?

11. What sort of reply would you expect Hester's letter to receive today? In what ways, if any, do you think attitudes have changed since it was written?

12. Why do you think the divorce law was different for men and for women? Is divorce equally easy for both sexes today?

Middle-class marriage p. 110:

13.   What do the extracts indicate about differences in married life for working-class women and middle-class women? For working-class men and middle-class men?

The double standard p. 113:

14.   How did the government committee justify the laws on prostitution? Do you think the attitudes expressed here still exist? If not, how have they changed?

The law and marriage about a hundred years ago p. 114:

15.   What in your opinion are the most important legal rights that women have gained over the last hundred years?

Staying single p. 115:

16.   Why do you think the 'old maids' in Salford were ridiculed? Do you think single men would have received the same treatment?

17.   Why was it considered so important for women of all classes to get married a hundred years ago?

18.   In what ways is the single life different for women today from a hundred years ago? Is there more pressure on women than men to marry today?

Modern marriage p. 116:

19.   From the evidence given, and from your own knowledge of married people, is marriage today a better deal for men or for women, or is it an equal partnership?

❧5❧

Having a family

'I am a mother of eleven children — six girls and five boys.
I was only nineteen years old when my first baby was
born . . . for twenty years I was nursing or expecting
babies.'
Margaret Llewelyn Davies (ed) *Maternity*
(referring to the 1890s)

In the 1880s and 90s the average number of children in a family was six, and to have eight, ten, or even twelve or more children was by no means uncommon. As well as bringing up large families, women gave birth to many more babies who didn't survive. One in five babies died at birth, and one in four died before they were one year old.

Most people had no access to any form of birth control. Throughout history people have tried to limit the number of children they have — it's not a new idea. But it is only in the last hundred years or so that effective contraceptives have been developed and in Britain this has changed both women's and men's lives enormously.

A PERFECT SLAVE

For most women, married life a hundred years ago was a succession of pregnancies and babies for perhaps twenty years or more:

'I was born in Bethnal Green, 9 April 1855, a tiny scrap of humanity.
I was my mother's seventh child, and seven more were born after
me — fourteen in all — which made my mother a perfect slave.
Generally speaking, she was either expecting a baby to be born or
had one at the breast. At the time there were eight of us the oldest

120

was not big enough to get ready to go to school without help.'
Mrs Layton, 'Memories of Seventy Years',
in Margaret Llewelyn Davies (ed) *Life As We Have Known It*

For working-class women the strain and hard work in having and bringing up such large families took its toll on their health and youth. They could not afford special care, or even take it easy, when pregnant. For example, many took on extra jobs to save up for the doctor's fee. There was no health service and to have a doctor attend the birth cost more than a week's wages in the 1880s. Many women were attended by a midwife — a very important person for women giving birth at this time; she cost less, but the money for a doctor would be needed if there were complications.

Maternity, a collection of letters from working-class women published in 1915, describes their experiences of pregnancy and childbirth. The following extracts from these letters illustrate the various hardships that women went through:

> 'One of the difficulties I experienced during pregnancy was saving the doctor's fee out of the small wage which was only just enough each week for ordinary expenses . . . Fancy bending over the washing-tub doing the family washing perhaps an hour or two before the baby is born.'

Many mothers had to get up and carry on immediately after having a baby when they were often not fit to do so:

> 'For many of my children I have not been able to pay a nurse to look after me, and I have got out of bed on the third day to make my own gruel and fainted away.'

" SHE WAS EITHER EXPECTING A BABY OR HAD
ONE AT THE BREAST. "

In most working-class families, money was too short to afford extra food during pregnancy. Many women were seriously undernourished and this affected the health of the baby:

> 'By that time hard work and worry and insufficient food had told on my once robust constitution, with the result that I nearly lost my life through want of nourishment, and did after nine months of suffering lose my child. No-one but mothers who have gone through the ordeal of pregnancy half starved, to finally bring a child into the world, to live a living death for nine months, can understand what it means.'

ANOTHER MOUTH TO FEED

In poor families the prospect of another child to feed and clothe was sometimes more of a worry than a pleasure:

> 'All the beautiful in motherhood is very nice if one has plenty to bring up a family on, but what real mother is going to bring a life into the world to be pushed into the drudgery of the world at the earliest possible moment because of the strain on the family exchequer.'
>
> Margaret Llewelyn Davies (ed) *Maternity*

A family making wire brushes (1890s)

A miner and his daughter having tea (1900s)

This was a great burden for men, who saw their families increasing but could do nothing to increase their earnings. One man remembers:

'I do know this, that every time a child was born it was a tragedy, owing to the poverty.'

John Langley, *Always a Layman*

One husband walked twelve miles a day to get to work and back in order to save the fares when his wife was pregnant. Another had to lose a day and a half's pay to look after her when she was in danger of losing the baby. His workmates had a whip-round and raised a pound for him. Many wives who wrote about the difficulties of having a large family, stressed how important it was to have a kind and considerate husband:

'My husband has been good in all my sickness. If he had not, I could not have lived through it.'

Maternity

WHAT COULD YOU DO?

It was very common for married women to try to give themselves abortions as the only way out of having an unwanted child. Some doctors at the time reckoned that one in four pregnancies ended in this way. There was no safe,

123

legal abortion available as there is today. Women simply tried well-known but dangerous methods; pints of gin, hot baths, knitting needles, falling downstairs. Worse still, many poisoned themselves by taking dangerous drugs, which brought on an abortion as a side-effect. For example, adhesive plasters could be bought from the chemist containing diachylon, which was made from lead. Women would eat the diachylon off the plaster, or make up a mixture like 'hickey-pickey', which was bitter apple, bitter aloes and white lead – a pennyworth of each from the chemist. A London woman, Mrs Matthews, remembers the everyday gossip:

> 'Someone would say "Oh she's going to have a baby, but she's trying to get rid of it. If she can't do the trick with a bottle of gin she'll try something stronger." It was quite common and it wasn't shocking or anything because who could blame them?'

The only contraceptives that could be bought until the 1880s were quite expensive and extremely difficult to find out about or obtain. They were not sold over the counter as they are today. They were not very reliable either. Women could use a small piece of sponge on a string soaked in a sperm-killing substance, called a pessary. For men there were sheaths ('French letters') made out of leather. By the 1880s rubber was used instead which meant that they were cheaper. Still the average man had no way of finding out about them and buying them.

A new invention of the 1880s was the 'Dutch Cap' for women. This is a round piece of rubber, which, when inserted, acts as a barrier against sperms. This method, still used today, was later to prove very important for women because it meant that they could take the initiative themselves and even use it without their husbands' knowing. But in the 1880s the Cap was not widely known.

The other methods of contraception most commonly used by women today, the Pill and the Coil, were not yet invented.

Contraceptives could not be advertised or openly displayed at all. The few chemists that supplied them could only circulate their price lists and catalogues privately, and to get these you had to write specially for them. So for most people the information was virtually inaccessible.

PRICE LIST FOR CONTRACEPTIVES 1886	
Sheaths	3/– a dozen
extra strong quality	5/– a dozen
Sponge & quinine pessary	2/– each
Dutch caps	2/3d, 2/6d, 3/– each
	(A. Lambert & Co, London)

Bringing up a baby in Bethnal Green (1890s)

'IN THE KNOW'

A large family did not mean such great hardship if you had plenty of money, but it still meant that women spent much of their lives having children. Queen Victoria, for example, had nine. Population statistics suggest that after the 1870s, middle-class people were starting to use contraception. These figures contrast the birth rate in middle-class Hampstead with that of working-class Shoreditch:

BIRTH RATE (births per 1000 people per year)		
1881	Hampstead	31.2
	Shoreditch	30.0
1911	Hampstead	17.5
	Shoreditch	30.2

The fall in the birth rate in Hampstead may have been due to a number of factors. Contraceptives cost money. Those with more time and better education were more likely to be 'in the know' than the majority of the population. Such people might have friends and neighbours who were doctors. They also had the privacy and comfort available to use the contraceptives once they had obtained them. It was much easier for a husband and wife to use birth control if they had their own warm bedroom with water for washing, than if they shared a room with their children and the water tap was at the end of the garden.

FORBIDDEN KNOWLEDGE

The reason for the secrecy surrounding birth control was that, in Victorian Britain, anything to do with sex was considered unmentionable and kept hidden. The subject was associated with sin and shame, and this belief was upheld by the Church, doctors and politicians. The influence of religion and the Church on morality and ideas of what was right and wrong were still very strong at the time. The idea of openly discussing sex was out of the question.

The naked body was never publicly seen. Nude statues were given fig leaves to make them less embarrassing; at the sea-side, both men and women wore bathing costumes that covered most of their body, and they changed in separate 'bathing machines' which then took them right out into the water to avoid any danger of being seen by members of the opposite sex. Even the word 'leg' was considered rude — polite people said 'limb' — and some even covered their piano legs with frills! One reason why it was very hard for women to study art or medicine was the fear that they would in the

A mother and children (1907)

process, have to see naked bodies. Medical students of the 1870s were instructed to look at the ceiling while examining women.

Many people remember how nakedness was avoided in the home. Brothers and sisters, and even many wives and husbands, never saw each other naked. There were no films or advertisements showing naked bodies as there are today, no magazine articles on sex, no mention of the subject by teachers.

THE FACTS OF LIFE

> 'When I reached a certain age all my mother told me was "Be careful and don't put your hands in cold water." That was all I was ever told about sex.'
> Elizabeth Roberts, 'Working Class Women in the North West'

Children were usually brought up without any information about sex either from home or school. Most people probably learnt from classmates, as many still do today, but it was much harder to find things out then. For example, very many girls started their periods without having any idea at all of what was happening. It was referred to as 'being unwell'. Many children had no idea whatsoever where their brothers and sisters came from. Probably their mother's long full skirts, and their rounded figures from constant childbearing, meant that pregnancy was not too obvious anyway:

> 'Each year my mother would have a new baby. This was always a great surprise to us. We would wake up one morning and my father would say "You have a new brother," or "You have a new sister," as the case may be. I think she had fourteen children altogether.'
> Grace Foakes, *My Part of the River*

" WELL I THINK IT'S **DEAD** COMMON, LOOK AT THE HEIGHT OF THAT HEMLINE ! "

Some women got married without any knowledge of sex at all. One woman remembers being told by her mother:

> 'After your wedding my dear, unpleasant things will happen to you but take no notice of them, I never did.'

Another wrote:

> 'I was very ignorant when I was married; my mother didn't consider it at all proper to talk about such things. There is too much mock modesty in the world.'
>
> Margaret Llewelyn Davies (ed) *Maternity*

Childbirth was another subject that wasn't discussed with daughters or single women and many women had no idea how a baby was born until it actually happened to them:

> 'I was married at twenty-eight in utter ignorance of the things that most vitally affect a wife and mother. My mother, dear, pious soul, thought ignorance was innocence and the only thing I remember her saying on the subject of childbirth was, "God never sends a baby without bread to feed it." Dame experience long ago knocked the bottom out of that argument for me.'
>
> *Maternity*

There were no classes on childbirth and no books or information available as there are today. While mothers said little or nothing to their daughters, married couples did not discuss the subject either. Men too, found it difficult to discuss these matters, and were often ignorant about them. Mr Forbes, a London man, remembers:

> 'You just didn't talk about that sort of thing in those days. We just knew to go for help when the time came. There was no question of the man being present at the birth like today.'

NATURAL INSTINCTS

Not only were women especially protected from knowing about sex, but they were believed by doctors to have no sexual feelings apart from the wish to have children. One well-known doctor wrote:

> 'As a general rule, a modest woman desires no sexual gratification for herself. She submits to her husband, but only to please him; and but for the desire for babies, would far rather be relieved from his attentions . . . The majority of women (happily for them) are not very much troubled with sexual feeling of any kind.'
>
> Dr Acton, 1876

For men, sex was believed to be a natural urge, but they were expected to

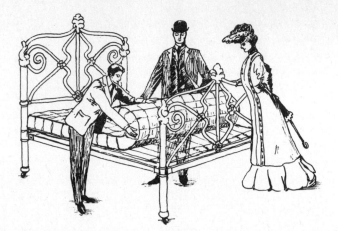

"......AND YOU, SIR, SLEEP HERE. WE GUARANTEE NO SATISFACTION OR CHILDREN !"

control it as far as possible. The same doctor advised that too much sex was harmful for men: 'Sperms are a man's vital substance − a kind of energy − and if all used up he will be unable to work to his full capacity.' He advised that once a week was the most that a man could safely have sex without damaging his health, and suggested that married men slept with their hands tied behind their backs to avoid temptation.

Other sorts of sexual activity were believed to be harmful:

> **'Many legends existed among us about masturbation, all aiming to warn against its dire effects, physical and mental. It was, we understood, the root cause in children of blindness, baldness, and galloping consumption.'**
>
> **Robert Roberts, *A Ragged Schooling***

Since girls were believed to have no sexual feelings, this was not seen as a female problem at all.

These are of course the views of doctors and medical writers, and it does not mean that ordinary men and women living at the end of the last century did not have good sexual relationships. What their statements do show, however, is that the general climate of 'respectable' opinion was one of disapproval when it came to sex. The very idea of being able to enjoy it without the 'natural' result of producing children was quite shocking and unacceptable to most people.

'THINK OF ENGLAND'

In Britain a hundred years ago, over-population was not seen as a world problem as it is today. Britain ruled a vast Empire which covered one-

130

quarter of the globe, providing huge markets for British goods. Working people were encouraged to have large families to provide the labour for British industry, which people believed would go on expanding. The wealthy felt it was their duty to produce children to be the future rulers of that Empire. The phrase 'Close your eyes and think of England' sums up what a middle-class mother might have advised her daughter about sex in marriage.

Holding the ruling position in the world meant that the British upper classes were inclined to believe that they were a superior 'race', and this was another encouragement to have children — to increase the number of 'good British stock'.

But one group, who called themselves 'Malthusians', after the writer Thomas Malthus, believed that the root cause of poverty was over-population. In particular, they believed that birth control was a good thing for the working classes, and that unhealthy, undernourished people should be prevented from breeding too many unhealthy, undernourished children. However, many people who were concerned about the poor did not see

Queen Victoria and her family (1894)

131

birth control as a solution to working-class poverty. They believed the answer lay in better housing, education, and higher wages.

THE REBELS

The few people who campaigned for birth control in the last century were rebels against the accepted ideas of the times. In 1820 Francis Place, a London tailor, wrote and gave out leaflets for working people, explaining simple methods of contraception. His leaflets were banned — the authorities called them 'The Diabolical Handbills' — meaning they were the work of the devil.

In 1860, Charles Bradlaugh founded the Malthusian League to spread knowledge about birth control. The League held public meetings and also distributed leaflets.

In 1877, Annie Besant and Charles Bradlaugh were arrested for publishing a book on birth control with illustrations called *The Fruits of Philosophy*. It actually said very little but was banned as a 'filthy dirty book'. Their trial attracted great publicity, and as a result thousands of copies of the book were sold.

In 1885, Dr Albutt published a book on baby care including a chapter on birth control. He was struck off the medical register for this. His book cost 6d (2½p), and he explained that there was nothing in it that was not contained in books costing £2. His crime was making the information available to the poor.

WHAT THE DOCTORS SAID

During the last century, most members of the medical profession fiercely opposed birth control. In the 1890s leading doctors argued that using contraceptives would produce 'A mania leading to suicide in women'. Men would suffer from 'mental decay, loss of memory, mania and conditions which lead to suicide'.

The Annual Medical Conference of 1883 stated: 'They are beastly contrivances for the prevention of conception.' Some doctors went as far as recommending methods that included no 'artificial' devices. One book in the 1890s recommended coughing, sneezing, jumping up and down, and violent exercise after intercourse.

Yet in spite of this opposition, ordinary people were beginning to want to know more, as this letter suggests:

> 'I know it is a most delicate subject, and very great care must be used in introducing it, but still, a word spoken sometimes does good. It is a delicate subject, but it is an urgent one, due to low-paid wages and the unearthly struggle to live respectably.'
>
> *Maternity*

By the beginning of this century, more people were becoming aware that it was possible to limit their families. When the first mass public meetings on birth control were held in the 1900s, big crowds turned out, eager for practical information.

MARIE STOPES

Marie Stopes was born into a middle-class home just over one hundred years ago in 1880, and was brought up in complete ignorance of sex. She became the most outstanding pioneer of the birth control movement. Today her ideas may not seem shocking, but in her own day she was a revolutionary who dared to bring the subject into the headlines. She knew from personal experience the unhappiness and suffering caused by widespread ignorance, and believed passionately that people had a right to a happy sex-life — particularly women.

Marie became the youngest Doctor of Science in Britain — a remarkable achievement for a woman. After her own marriage it took her three years to realise something was wrong — she and her husband had never made love. She only found out what was missing by going to the British Museum and reading books on the subject. After her marriage ended, she was determined to help others whose ignorance ruined their marriages.

In 1918 she published a book called *Married Love* with this aim:

> 'It would be a book on marriage and sex and it would teach a man and woman how to understand each other's sexual problems. It would not be presented as a scientific book, or it would defeat its purpose to help ordinary people who require a book simply, even emotionally written.'
>
> Marie Stopes, *Married Love*

She used plain language for the first time in a book about sex. It sold 2000 copies in the first fortnight alone, and she became a household name:

> 'Jeanie, Jeanie, full of hopes,
>   Read a book by Marie Stopes,
> Now, to judge by her condition,
>   She must have read the wrong edition.'
>   (Popular rhyme)

She had answered a real need in people, understanding what problems they faced:

> 'The idea that woman is lowered by sex-intercourse is very deeply rooted in our present society . . . Both law and custom have strengthened the view that he has the right to approach his wife whenever he wishes, and that she has no wishes and no needs in the

133

matter at all . . . After a few months or maybe a few years of marriage they seem to have drifted apart, and he finds her often cold.'

Marie Stopes, *Married Love*

She explained that women do have feelings too, and helped men to understand them.

In response, people wrote to her from all over the country with their problems which, until then, they had had to keep so secret. These letters show how difficult things often were for men as well as women: From a vicar:

'We go to rest, my wife always lies with her back towards me, I make a tender advance and suggest that she turn around so that we may chat and cuddle – the end of the poetry is "I do not like your breath in my face" . . . I fear my loved one has known no rapture.'

Another vicar wrote:

'She is slow to rouse, once or twice a year, possibly four times, I find heaven in her unspeakable sweet joy. Can it be oftener? Can it be fairly regular?'

From a soldier:

'My wife considered all bodily desire to be nothing less than animal passion, and that true love between husband and wife should be purely mental and not physical. This naturally caused a split in our married life and now we are separated . . . like so many English-women she considered that any show of affection was not in keeping with her dignity as a woman, and that all lovemaking and caresses should come entirely from the man.'

From a teacher:

'I have been reading again your beautiful book 'Married Love' and it has filled me with intense sadness. For it has made me realise all the joy of marriage that I have missed . . . I found my wife more and more reluctant to receive me. So it is now more than four years since we have had any intercourse.'

Ruth Hall, *Dear Dr Stopes*

Women wrote too, showing how the fear of pregnancy was the cause of much unhappiness:
From an ex-nurse with four children:

'I am so afraid of conception that I cannot bear for my husband to even speak kindly to me or even put his hand on my shoulder for fear

134

Mary Stopes and the nurses at the first birth control clinic

he wants his rights and it causes a lot of anger and misery. It is two months since I last allowed him intercourse.'

The next letter is from a woman who badly wanted to have children and whose husband went to the doctor for an examination:

'My husband was told to go for a six month holiday without me and eat oysters and drink stout and probably things would come right. We are not well off, so of course he couldn't leave his work for all that time and he hates eating oysters. Trusting you will help us . . .'

Another husband wrote:

'I think I may honestly claim to have at all times tried to have been the thoughtful and tenderly careful husband that you so rightly instruct one to be. For instance I honestly thought, as do most clean-living men, that one ought never to have connections after one was aware that conception had commenced. I went further than this; I thought that at least one year should elapse after childbirth . . . I found the restraint increasingly difficult.'

Ruth Hall, *Dear Dr Stopes*

THE FIRST CLINIC

In 1921, Marie Stopes opened the first birth control clinic in Holloway, a working-class area of London. Like the Malthusian League, Marie believed that the poor should be discouraged from having children, but at the same time, she showed understanding of their situation. At her clinic advice was given free, and contraceptives – usually the 'cap' for women – were sold at cost price, the price often being waived for the very poor. The clinic was run by nurses and a midwife instead of a doctor which helped many women who felt they could not talk to a man. One of the first patients wrote:

'I belong to the working class and know only too well how bitterly the working classes need the help Dr Marie Stopes is giving . . . I thank God every day that I visited the Clinic when I did . . . What do our lives become? we get broken in health, have sickly babies and too often have to go out to work to make ends meet. And our poor husbands have to suffer for it, you nag at them and then they pay toll at the nearest public house. I wish Dr Marie Stopes was a multi-millionaire so that she could open clinics in every town in England.'

Ruth Hall, *Dear Dr Stopes*

A record was kept of the first five thousand patients who attended:
4170 women were fitted with 'caps'
57 men were provided with sheaths
324 women were given pessaries

Case histories were also kept:

'*B.2* Husband unfaithful because wife denied unions for fear of pregnancy.
B.8 Seventeen pregnancies, ten living. Husband and wife can neither read nor write.
B.7 Has had four confinements in two years – three dead.
B.14 Has had six criminal abortions.
E.8 Has had seventeen pregnancies and seven living children. Quarrels with husband regarding too frequent unions. The only time she was happy was when her husband was away at the war.

E.6 In two years has had three premature babies, one miscarriage and an operation for appendicitis.

G.15 Only 28 years of age and has had nine pregnancies, consisting of three living children, one dead and five miscarriages.

G.20 Twelve pregnancies. One child died and one induced abortion. Husband Roman Catholic and refused to take any precautions.'

Marie Stopes, *The First Five Thousand*

As well as running the clinic, Marie Stopes devoted her life to the cause of birth control at this time. She wrote many other books and articles in newspapers to get publicity. She held many meetings, even travelling in a mobile caravan to spread the word. She aroused furious opposition. This is what some of her opponents had to say:

Blackie, (the publishers, who declined her book):
'I think there is far too much talking and writing about these things already.'

Dr Wheeler, a scientist (on reading her book):
'It is the insistence on the animalism of the act of sex-relation which has aroused my anger . . . I mentioned before the ugliness of many of the words you have chosen – "orgasm", "ejaculation" and so forth.'

The Bishop of Southwark:
'The only thing that justifies ultimately the intercourse between man and woman is the purpose and the desire to have children.'

Opposition came from women as well:

Mrs Booth (co-founder of the Salvation Army):
'Young girls are being destroyed in great numbers each year because of it [the book].'

Catholic Women's Guild:
'It will lead to race suicide and moral degeneracy.'

from Ruth Hall, *Marie Stopes*

Despite these attacks, more and more women went to the clinic.

THE MOVEMENT GROWS

As we have seen, the movement for birth control, which started towards the end of the nineteenth century, did not influence great numbers of people until after the First World War. By 1925 there were six clinics outside London as well as two in London, all privately run but inexpensive and aimed at helping working-class women. The number of pioneers increased.

Margaret Sanger, who was arrested in New York for opening a clinic, came to England in 1914. Dora Russell and Stella Browne toured the country in the early 1920s speaking to packed meetings of working-class women who came surrounded by babies and toddlers. Dr Helena Wright, who ran a London clinic from 1928, found that people were astonished when given information: 'Oh, really! Can it really be done?' they asked her. Even doctors started to change their opinions when Lord Dawson, the King's doctor, declared in a speech to Bishops in 1921:

> 'Birth control is here to stay. It is an established fact and, for good or evil, has to be accepted . . . No denunciations will abolish it.'

Of course this shocked some — the headline in the next edition of the *Sunday Express* was 'Lord Dawson must go!'

The newly-formed Labour party was forced into giving its support by its women members in the Women's Co-operative Guild and the Labour Women's Conference. A Workers' Birth Control Group was formed to put pressure on the government to take action. By 1930, even the Bishops of the Church of England had decided that it was all right to provide information about birth control.

STATE SUPPORT

Birth control has become widely available today because the state now provides a service. This has only recently become the case. At first, the government, as well as the medical professions, were opposed to providing any information or help on birth control. When the first mothers' clinics were set up after the First World War, health visitors were forbidden to give any advice on the subject. A London nurse was dismissed from her job for doing just this. A woman who worked as a health visitor at the time remembers:

> 'I had strict instructions that I was to give no information about birth control under any condition. I'd have got the sack. If people asked I told them I couldn't tell them anything, but if they went down to the Clinic in Walworth they could find out everything they needed.'

Many of the local health authorities opposed the voluntary birth control clinics, but in spite of this the number of clinics increased, as did their attendance figures. In 1930 the various groups joined together as the National Birth Control Council — later it became the Family Planning Association — to put more pressure on local councils. Gradually, in the 1930s, local authorities started to loan out premises for family planning, and to allow information to be given out in their own health clinics when further pregnancies were believed to be bad for the mother's health.

In the ten years between 1925 and 1935, the number of voluntary clinics increased from 8 to 47, and a further 66 clinics were opened under the local health authorities. Over the last 50 years, largely thanks to the work of the Family Planning Association, the number of clinics gradually increased, and the services provided by them expanded including helping the unmarried with contraceptive advice and those unable to have children. Breaking down prejudice was a very long and slow battle and many people can remember how things were still very secretive in the 1940s and 1950s. Many women used contraceptives without ever mentioning it to their husbands. Barber shops were for a long time the only places in many areas where men could buy contraceptives. And it was not until 1967 that all local authorities were instructed by the government to provide a family planning service as part of local health provision.

PLANNED FAMILIES

Since the 1950s, new and more effective methods of contraception have been developed, though none of them has as yet been perfected by any means. The most important of these are the Pill, the coil (or IUD) the cap and sterilisation for both men and women. The Pill, coil and cap have enabled women to take full responsibility for birth control, deciding whether or not to have children, and how many.

Equally important, contraception is easily available in this country and is either cheap or provided free of charge under the National Health Service. Contraceptives can be bought over the counter in chemists, obtained free from clinics, or on prescription from a doctor.

Attitudes towards sex and birth control have changed enormously especially in the last ten or twenty years. For example, men are more often involved in visits to family planning clinics, and many are now having vasectomies (male sterilisation). Couples now talk about the subject, rather than being too shy to discuss it. It is often still very difficult to discuss sex with parents and older people, but it is easier today to get information if you want it, and most schools provide at least some sex education. Another very important change is that advice and help is available to unmarried people and those under sixteen.

However, the ideal or perfect contraceptive does not yet exist. Some women, for example, suffer from unpleasant side effects or discomfort from the Pill, and it is not suitable for all women. The coil is not always effective or completely safe, and while the sheath has no side effects it can be awkward for a couple and is not as reliable as other methods.

Sometimes new contraceptive methods have been used without sufficient trial and testing, especially in underdeveloped countries, with harmful effects on women.

There are still, in this country, many unwanted pregnancies: the Family

Planning Association estimated that about 130,000 unplanned babies were born each year in the late 1970s. About half of all teenage brides are already pregnant when they get married.

Since 1967 when a new law was passed, abortion, which is now safe and quick, has been available under the National Health Service. Yet many women who want abortions cannot have them, either because there is not enough provision where they live, or because of opposition from their doctors. There is still considerable opposition to the principle of abortion, and there have been many attempts to reverse the 1967 law and make abortion less available – especially to people who can't afford to pay large amounts of money for it. There are still women in Britain today who die as a result of having an illegal and dangerous abortion. So although birth control has become accepted, and families are smaller as a result, we have not yet reached a situation in which, as the National Abortion Campaign demands, 'Every child is a wanted child and every mother a willing mother.'

QUESTIONS
'A perfect slave' p. 120:
1.   Judging from these extracts, in what ways did frequent childbearing affect women's health? Does it have the same effects today?

2.   How did financial hardship affect having a baby? Does it affect working people in the same way today?

Another mouth to feed p. 122:
3.   How were men able to help their wives when they were having babies? What can they do today to help?

4.   The extracts here emphasise the hardships involved in having a large family. What do you think the advantages might have been?

What could you do? p. 123:
5.   Why did women use dangerous methods to have abortions? How can a woman get an abortion today?

'In the know' p. 126:
6.   What do the photographs show about the differences between wealthy and working-class families?

7.   What evidence is there to suggest that middle-class people were more likely to find out about, and use, contraception than working-class people?

Forbidden knowledge p. 126:
8.   How far would you say that attitudes about sex and nakedness have changed over the past century? Have they changed for the better or worse?

The facts of life p. 128:

9. From reading these extracts, do you think we are much better informed than people were a hundred years ago?

Natural instincts p. 129:

10. What do Dr Acton's views tell us about attitudes towards women and men at that time? In what ways do you think these ideas have changed today?

'Think of England' p. 130:

11. Why do you think attitudes towards population have changed in Britain since the nineteenth century?

The rebels p. 132:

12. What exactly was it these 'rebels' did that got them into trouble? Why do you think it was an offence to give birth control information to the poor but not to the rich? What issues do people get into trouble for when they speak out about them in this country today?

Marie Stopes p. 133:

13. Judging from the letters here, why do you think Marie Stopes became so well known?

The first clinic p. 136:

14. Why was the opening of a clinic such an important step in the spread of birth control? Do you think it was a wise policy to have midwives working there instead of doctors?

15. What do the case studies tell us about marriage and family life before the existence of widespread birth control?

16. Why was there such strong opposition to Marie Stopes, as indicated in the extracts here?

The movement grows p. 137:

17. Why had birth control become more accepted by the 1930s?

State support p. 138:

18. Why do you think the state was so opposed to the spread of birth control at this time? Why had attitudes changed by the 1960s?

Planned families p. 139:

19. What are the benefits and drawbacks of modern birth control? What are the arguments for and against making abortion more easily available?

20. In what ways do you think attitudes have changed since the end of the last century towards contraception? Do you think people today are influenced by the ideas of a hundred years ago?

❧6❧

Running the home

'A man's job in those days was not in the house; they came home at six and that was the end of it. I never saw my father do a thing in the house and I never saw him go shopping or carrying a shopping bag. The women never stopped working — they worked themselves to death.'
A London housewife, born 1901

A hundred years ago housework was a much harder and more time-consuming job than today. All the cleaning was done by hand, which meant hours of scrubbing and heavy lifting. All food and all cleaning materials had to be made in the home — there were no ready-made, frozen meals and no bottles of instant cleaner. All this work was done by women. A man might garden or clean the shoes, but housework was women's work. For working men had to put in a very long and hard day's work to support their families. Therefore, they didn't expect to have to work when they got home as well.

Running a home was a different matter if you were rich enough to employ servants, but here again it was the women servants who did the housework. Male servants looked after the horses, drove the carriage and opened the front door, but they didn't cook, wash or clean. Even modest, middle-class homes usually had one female servant — a 'maid of all work' as they were called.

THE HOUSE

Victorian houses were hard to clean. The fashion was to have lots of shelves and ledges, mantelpieces, skirting boards, moulded ceilings — all places where dust could collect easily. Furniture was very large and heavy to move.

A prosperous, working-class family might have a small house to themselves, but poorer families were often crowded into one or two rooms. Housework must have been particularly inconvenient when there was no space to store things, when beds had to be made up in the living room and people were running in and out. In some houses there were mice, rats and bugs to contend with too:

> 'The question of vermin is a very pressing one in all the small houses. No woman, however clean, can cope with it . . . the mothers accept the pest as part of their dreadful lives but they do not grow reconciled to it. Repapering and fumigation are as far as any landlord goes in dealing with the difficulty.'
>
> Maud Pember Reeves, *Round About a Pound a Week*

A large percentage of the population lived in bad housing and there was no alternative — no council flats, no housing advice centres and no laws to protect tenants. To buy a house was completely beyond the reach of working people, so most families rented rooms. This cost about 3/− to 6/− a week (15−30p) — about a quarter to a third of the average working-class family's income.

Furniture to fill a two-roomed house cost £12−12s (£12. 60p) in the early 1900s	£	s	d
Leather couch or sofa	1	6	0
One hardwood armchair		9	6
One hardwood rocking chair		9	6
Four best kitchen chairs		15	6
One square table		10	6
3½ x 4 yards oil cloth		14	0
One cloth hearth rug		4	9
One kitchen fender		6	6
One set kitchen fire irons		4	6
One ash pan		2	11
One full-size brass mounted bedstead	1	12	6
One double woven wire mattress		14	6
One flock bed bolster and pillows		16	6
3ft 6in enclosed dressing table with fixed glass	1	15	
Wash stand with tile back	1	9	0
Two cane seat chairs		7	0
2½ x 4 yards oil cloth		10	0
Two bedside rugs		3	10
TOTAL	**12**	**12s**	**0d**

Robert Roberts, *The Classic Slum*

143

NO MOD CONS

Most working-class houses had only cold running water from one tap in the kitchen or yard which meant carrying buckets of water up and down stairs to wash. Sharing a house often meant going down to a neighbour's kitchen or walking through their rooms to get to the yard. Few homes had bathrooms, or the newly-invented gas 'geyser' to heat water. Working people had to boil their water in pots and kettles, and a bath was a weekly event when they squeezed into a tin tub in front of the fire, sharing the water with the rest of the family.

> **'A woman with six children under thirteen gives them all a bath with two waters between them on Saturday morning in the wash tub. She generally has a bath herself on Sunday evening when her husband is out. All the water has to be carried upstairs, heated in her kettle, and carried down again when dirty. Her husband baths when he can afford twopence, at the public baths.'**
>
> **Maud Pember Reeves, *Round About a Pound a Week***

If you had an out-house or scullery for doing the washing, you could bath inside the 'copper'. This was a big copper-lined stone stove for boiling water, heated by lighting a pile of wood underneath it. Mrs Murray, a Derbyshire housewife, explained:

> **'I used to bath all my brothers and sisters in the copper. I would boil it up, then leave it so that the bottom wasn't too hot. I'd sit them on the side and soap them all over with pieces cut off from a big bar of Sunlight soap, then dip them in the copper.'**

Everyday washing meant a wash-down with carbolic soap or soda from an enamel bowl on the kitchen table or a wash stand. Before the invention of toothpaste, people used tins of tooth powder, or just salt.

The toilet was outside, often at the end of the garden, so it was common to keep a chamber pot under the bed. A Lancashire man remembered:

> **'In the middle of winter you weren't going to risk pneumonia by running out in the night, so it was just the normal thing to do. The first job my mother did every morning was to go round with a pail and empty all the pots and clean them with carbolic.'**

Toilets were different, too. The modern 'wash down' design that's cleaned automatically with water had only been invented in the 1880s. Most people had the kind you had to tip water into and scrub clean after using. Many houses had no mains drainage so there would be an open sewer outside, near the house, which often smelt bad and was unhygienic. In some areas, there was danger that the water supply could become infected, as a government report on working-class housing in 1884 found:

'In Clerkenwell there are cases, as described, where there is not more than one closet for sixteen houses . . . in St Luke's closets were found in the cellars in a most disgraceful state of filth and stench, and close to the water supply.'

Royal Commission on the Housing of the Working Class

GAS LIGHTS AND COAL FIRES

A hundred years ago the most up-to-date lighting was the new gas lamp, gloomy by our standards and also dirty, making a dark ring on the ceiling above. Gas mantles could be bought — little pieces of fabric that burned in the gas flame to give a brighter light. Here is Mrs Matthew's memory of this kind of lighting:

'It was very fiddly. You had to keep buying new mantles and then you had to fit a glass shade over that. Even then you could only see to read if you sat right underneath it. Gas burned up the pennies, so to save the gas we used a candle in the bedroom. The hallway and toilet had no light, so we put a paraffin lamp on the wall.'

Heating was by coal fires which had to be cleared out and lit every morning. This was no easy job in a cold draughty house, first thing in the morning.

The following instructions were written for housemaids whose job it was:

'The fire is laid by first placing cinders, rather apart, at the bottom of the grate; then a piece of paper — not coarse brown, which will smoulder — and then a few crossbars of pieces of wood which should be kept well dried. On the wood some rubbly coals — not too close together, for a draught is required to kindle the fuel . . . light with a lucifer match.'

Warner's Model Cookery Book, 1890

Coal fires also meant carting heavy coals up flights of stairs, and they gave off thick black dust which settled all around the house.

CLEANING

The carpet sweeper had just been invented a hundred years ago but the vacuum cleaner was still a thing of the future. Most working people had rugs made at home out of rags. Carpets had to be brushed by hand — the best method was one using tea leaves. A London woman explains this method of carpet cleaning:

'You sprinkled your old tea leaves over the mat and they absorbed the bits of dust — then it's easier to sweep it up. But you weren't considered a good housewife unless you took your mats down to the yard, put them on the washing line and beat the life out of them.'

Jobs done outside did at least provide the chance to chat to neighbours:

> 'The morning cleaning proceeded to the accompaniment of neighbourly greetings and shouting across garden and fence; for the first sound of the banging of mats was a signal for others to bring out theirs, and it would be "Have 'ee heard of this?" and "War d'ye think of that?" '
>
> Flora Thompson, *Lark Rise to Candleford*

Many homes had lino on the floor or just bare boards, which had to be scrubbed, as Mrs Matthews explains:

> 'You bought a bottle of liquid carbolic for scrubbing − it was strong stuff and really smelt − I used to scrub the stairs so hard they went white and they curved in the middle because of the tread − today the carpets take the tread.'

There were no rubber gloves, so scrubbing made hands red raw from the harsh chemicals like soda and carbolic. Scrubbing also led to backache. Dusting may not be a hard job today, but with coal fires and no vacuum cleaners it was a different matter. As one woman explained: 'You couldn't get rid of the dust − you just moved it from one place to the next − as you swept it off the floor you watched it settling on the mantelpiece.'

The middle-class fashion was to have a great many ornaments, all of which attracted dust. In the kitchen, china was kept on a dresser made of open wooden shelves, and had to be regularly taken down and washed.

Kitchen surfaces were made of wood or marble which needed hard scrubbing, and the cleaner made up at home:

> 'To clean marble; take ¼ pint pure soap, ½ gill turps., pipe clay, bullocks' gall, mix to a paste and use as polish.'
>
> Mrs Beeton, *Book of Household Management*

CLEANLINESS IS NEXT TO GODLINESS

Great importance was attached to keeping the front of the house spotless. Cleanliness was seen as a sign of respectability and many people took the saying that 'cleanliness is next to godliness' very much to heart:

> 'Women wore their lives away washing clothes in heavy iron-hooped tubs, scrubbing wood and stone, polishing furniture and fire-irons. On Saturday mornings steps and pavements were cleaned to show their cleanliness to the world.'
>
> Robert Roberts, *The Classic Slum*

The front steps were whitened with hearthstone which was bought in a

147

Helping mother on wash day (1903)

large lump. One London housewife regarded this job as a privilege when she was young: 'My ambition was to clean the front steps for my mother . . . I knew I would feel so proud, but first I had to show that I could scrub the rest of the house.' But to a servant it was a chore:

> '**Nowadays if you do hearthstone your steps, and not many people do, you can buy it in a packet of powder, but we used to have a big lump like a beach stone and had to rub it hard on the steps. There you were in a sacking apron with your bottom sticking out and the errand boys throwing cheeky remarks at you.**'
>
> **Margaret Powell,** *Below Stairs*

Door knobs and knockers were made of brass which had to be kept shining bright. There were also brass stair rods, taps, finger plates and handles, ornaments and dishes for those who could afford them — all of which required regular cleaning. For the hard up, cleaning materials were one thing that could be economised on, which made housework even harder:

> '**Two pennyworth of soap may have to wash the clothes, scrub the**

floors, and wash the people of a family for a week. It is difficult to realise the soap famine in such a household. Soda, being cheap, is made to do a great deal. It sometimes appears in the children's weekly bath; it often washed their hair. A woman who had been using her one piece of soap to scrub the floor next brought it into play when she bathed the baby.'

Maud Pember Reeves, *Round About a Pound a Week*

WASHING UP

Saucepans were made of heavy iron or copper, and cooking over a coal stove made them black with soot and hard to clean:

'A pet hate was cleaning the copper saucepans. Every time they were used they got filthy. All the bright polish would be tarnished after every meal. They had to be cleaned with a horrible mixture of silver sand, salt, vinegar and a little flour. You mixed all this into a paste and then rubbed it in with your bare hands. You couldn't put it on with rags because you couldn't get the pressure that way . . . it was a foul job. Every morning I had to do it.'

Margaret Powell, *Below Stairs*

Washing up was done with Hudson's soda, and all the water had to be boiled up:

'The sinks were shallow stone ones, a dark grey in colour, made of cement. They were porous, not glazed china or stainless steel like you get now, and the dirty water sort of saturated into them and they stank to high heaven. That washing up was what you'd call a chore these days.'

Margaret Powell, *Below Stairs*

Cutlery was not made of stainless steel, as it is today, but of iron which rusted, and so it had to be cleaned carefully. Spoons and forks were rubbed with brickdust, and knives on a knife board with emery paper.

WASHING AND IRONING

Mrs Murray, a Derbyshire housewife, describes wash day in a working-class home at the turn of the century:

'Wash day was a whole day's work. First of all you sorted out your whites from your coloureds and put them all in to soak. Then you gave everything a good scrub with a brush on a washboard, especially the collars and cuffs. Then you boiled up the whites in the copper, poking them down all the time with a wooden stick and plenty of soap – pieces cut off a big block. After that you rinsed and

Two maids doing the washing with a 'dolly' washing machine (1910)

blued them – you put a "bluebag" into the water to bring the whites up white. Then the coloureds had to be done, everything rinsed and put through the mangle. Then out on the line to dry. Then you had to clean out the copper and scrub it ready for next time.'

Washing machines were unknown to most people until well into this century. As one woman put it: 'I didn't know anyone who had a washing machine – the old woman was a washing machine and she ran on elbow grease.' The machines that were on the market by the 1880s, for those who could afford them, still had to be worked by hand – they consisted of a wooden tub with a handle fixed to the lid which had to be turned to move the clothes about; it was called a 'dolly'. The only gadget most people had was a mangle for wringing out water between heavy rollers.

Starching was another part of the routine. The collars and cuffs of men's shirts, tablecloths and pillowcases were all starched by boiling them separately in starch powder. There were more items around the house that needed washing too – the fashion was for runners and doilies on shelves, cupboards and chairbacks, and drapes on the mantelshelf. In the days before Terylene, curtains were made of white lace. Mrs Murray again: 'Washing the curtains was a whole day's work – they got so dirty you soaked them in starch to dissolve the dirt; then you had to pull them into shape and iron them.'

Irons were heavy and had to be heated on the stove and kept hot by reheating. Without today's non-iron and crease-resistant materials there was much more ironing to be done, and people were more fussy about ironing *all* their household linen then than they are now.

MENDING

Every woman had to darn and mend in her spare time. Socks and stockings were made of wool which went into holes far more easily than today's synthetic fibres. Clothes were patched and mended again and again to make them last as long as possible. A Lancashire woman remembers her mother darning:

'She used to re-foot our stockings; when they got too full of holes to be darned any more she would cut the foot out of another old stocking and sew it in. With the men's socks she knitted on a new foot. The trouble was it used to rub your feet.'

There were no cleaners' shops, so all the cleaning and repair jobs we now pay for were done at home. The man usually mended all the family's shoes. He could buy leather pieces and cut out heels and soles to fit each size:

'One man, a printer's handyman, spends some time every day over the boots of his children. He is a steady, intelligent man, and he says it takes him all his spare time. As soon as he has gone round the family the first pair is ready again.'

Maud Pember Reeves, *Round About a Pound a Week*

COOKING

Cooking was done on an iron 'range', or 'kitchener' as it was called, which was a coal stove with ovens built into the sides and hot plates on top. It was hard work keeping it clean, as Mrs Potts, from Lancashire, remembers:

'You had to rub it hard with blacklead to keep it black – otherwise it went rusty. You made up your blacklead from turps. and linseed oil, then rubbed it over the whole thing, then polished it until it shone. You took a great pride in keeping your kitchener shining.'

Gas cookers were just coming on to the market in the 1880s. They cost about £5 – over a month's wages – so few people could afford to buy one outright. Instead, they could have a penny-in-the-slot meter and pay in instalments. These stoves had many ledges where the grease collected. They too were cleaned with blacklead. But in some homes there was neither a range nor a stove:

'The certainty of an economical stove or fireplace is out of the reach of the poor. They are often obliged to use old-fashioned and broken ranges and grates which devour coal with as little benefit to the user as possible.'

Maud Pember Reeves, *Round About a Pound a Week*

One way round this problem was to take the Sunday dinner, the main cooked meal of the week, to the local baker's where it could be cooked. One baker in the 1880s offered to bake loaves for ¼d (⅛p), cakes on Fridays for 1d (½p), Sunday dinners for 2d (1p) and a turkey at Christmas for a shilling (5p).

In the country there might be a communal oven used by all the women:

'The womenfolk seemed to arrange their work together on washing days and baking days. On Mondays clouds of steam would pour out of the communal outhouse and on baking days lovely smells of fresh baked bread and cakes, which they would carry to their cottages on huge trays.'

George Noakes, *To be a Farmer's Boy*

Often the main meal of the day was some kind of stew, which would feed a large family economically, and this had to be prepared hours in advance. Mrs Matthews remembers her mother's cooking:

'My mother used to make us a cooked dinner every day – things like stew from a pennyworth of pieces and pot herbs – that's carrot and onion, or homemade meat pies and puddings – you couldn't buy them then. The dinner was put on in the morning to be ready when we came home at midday, and that was it – we never had deserts. Breakfast wasn't cooked – just bread and jam or dripping. You only had an egg on Sunday as a treat. Sunday was the big cook up . . . a joint of beef, batter pudding, roast potatoes and cabbage, and while the oven was on my mother made dozens of jam tarts and a big cake. That lasted us until Tuesday . . . then there was no more cake until the next Sunday.'

The kitchen range in a working-class home (1900s)

Here is one working-class family's diet in the 1900s. The amounts are for two adults and three children:	
SUNDAY	*Breakfast* – Half a loaf, butter and tea. *Dinner* – Roast mutton, potatoes, greens. *Tea* – Half a loaf, butter, tea, 2d cake for him.
MONDAY	*Breakfast* – Half a loaf, rolled oats with tinned milk. *Dinner* – Cold meat cooked up with onions, carrots, greens and potatoes. *Tea* – Half a loaf, jam and tea.
TUESDAY	*Breakfast* – Half a loaf, jam and tea. *Dinner* – Mutton chops, potatoes, greens. *Tea* – Half a loaf, butter and tea. Fish for him.
WEDNESDAY	*Breakfast* – Half a loaf, butter and cocoa. *Dinner* – 1lb pieces stewed with rice, carrots, onions, potatoes. *Tea* – Half a loaf, butter and tea. Fish for him.
THURSDAY	*Breakfast* – Half a loaf, tea, rolled oats and milk. *Dinner* – Boiled neck of mutton, rice, onions, greens, potatoes. *Tea* – Half a loaf, jam and tea. Fish for him.
FRIDAY	*Breakfast* – Half a loaf, butter and tea. *Dinner* – Suet pudding and treacle. *Tea* – Half a loaf, jam and tea.
SATURDAY	*Breakfast* – Half a loaf, butter and tea. *Dinner* – Eggs and bacon. *Tea* – Half a loaf, butter and tea.

Maud Pember Reeves, *Round About a Pound a Week*

Cooks and maids who worked in the kitchens of large houses, preparing more complicated meals, had tedious preparation to do – for example, making mince by hand with a sieve:

'The worst job of the lot was when they had minced beef cake. The raw beef, generally a fillet, had to go through the mincer. That wasn't easy. But then I had to get it through a wire sieve, still raw, so you can imagine how long this took. I thought it was impossible when I first tried, but I found I could do it if I kept on long enough.'

Margaret Powell, *Below Stairs*

Baking bread in a communal oven, Emmaville Colliery (1904)

Crisps were home-made by deep frying. Soups were made by first, boiling bones for 24 hours to make stock, then chopping, simmering, straining and sieving vegetables. The first tinned foods became available in the 1880s but were not common. In any case the poor couldn't afford them, and the rich preferred their cook's handiwork.

SHOPPING

For ordinary people, shopping meant buying little and often. A London woman remembered her childhood in the 1890s:

> 'We had no food at all in store, there was nowhere to keep it even if you could have afforded to go and spend. The only thing that came in tins was jam and we never had a tin. Us kids were sent along with a saucer for a pennyworth. We all went to market on Saturday nights – then they were practically giving the food away. It was drummed into us always to buy small amounts – a pennyworth of anything at a time was all you could afford.'

Some working-class men were paid on a daily basis, so their wives had to wait until they got home before they could go and buy the food. It was usual to 'run short' before a weekly pay day. One London man remembered his mother's way of coping:

Waiting for the pawnshop to open (1880s)

'She would pray the gas meter wouldn't run out on a Wednesday because she only had a couple of shillings left to get the dinners until Friday. She would think up the cheapest dinners and if that didn't work, she'd have to borrow off my Gran.'

One solution for the housewife was to buy on 'trust' from the local corner-shop where she was known. The debt was written in the 'trust book' and had to be paid at the end of the week before more goods could be bought on 'trust' for the next week. Alternatively, there was the pawnshop, where belongings like a bundle of clothes could be exchanged for cash. They were kept until the customer could afford to go and claim them. In the 1890s a man's suit fetched 2/− (10p) plus an extra 3d (1½p) to get it back. A weekly trip to the pawnbroker's was a regular feature in some homes. Mrs Halls, a railway worker's daughter, remembered:

'Every Monday I had to take a parcel in and then collect it at the end of the week. It was my father's suit, which he only wore when he went out to the pub at weekends. He didn't know about this, but on the weeks when my mother couldn't afford to pay to get it out she had to deliberately pick a row with him so that they would both be in too bad a mood to go for a drink and he would never know.'

SHOPS AND STREET SELLERS

Shops themselves were very different from today. Goods weren't ready-packaged and there was no self-service, as Mrs Potts remembers:

'You bought your butter in pats cut from a huge slab in the grocer's. Biscuits were weighed up in big tins, and you could buy half a pound of broken biscuits very cheaply; tea and coffee, even sugar was weighed up for you in the shop on scales, and the coffee was always ground – there was no instant. With all these things in big sacks the shop smelt fantastic.'

Many household items came from the 'oil shop' — rather like today's hardware store. Here people bought paraffin for oil lamps, cleaning materials such as soda in penny lumps, and chunks of green soap cut off a huge block and wrapped in newspaper.

A common sight was the many street traders who came around to people's houses, selling food. Milk was ladled out of a churn into people's own jugs. The baker, fishman, cocklewoman and winkleseller all came round at certain times of the week. On Sundays, the muffin man came round ringing a bell and people bought muffins for their Sunday tea along with watercress and celery from the cresslady. The rag man offered pieces of odd china for old rags and the iron man would buy scrap iron for a few pence.

The rabbit seller (1900)

MANAGING

The physical work was only part of the business of running a home. Managing the money was also the woman's job — not an easy one for the one-third of the population who were earning too little to live on. Here's one woman's budget in the early 1900s:

	shillings	pence		shillings	pence
rent	6	6	husband's dinners	3	0
insurance	1	0	bread	3	4½
gas		6	1lb dripping		6
coal		8½	12oz butter		9
wood		2	8oz tea		8
soap & soda		5	2 tins milk		6
cleaning powder		1	meat	2	3
baby's soap		2	potatoes		3
			vegetables		6
			flour		3
			bloaters (kippers)		2
			suet		2
			3lb sugar		6
TOTAL	9s	6½d	TOTAL	12s	10½d

Maud Pember Reeves, *Round About a Pound a Week*

This family's total income was 22s 6d a week — reckoned at the time to be just about enough to survive on without any extras — so at the end of the week this family had 1d to spare. Here are some prices at that time:

Bacon	6d a pound (2½p)
Sunday joint	1/- (5p)
Sausages	4d a pound (2p)
Fish	4d a pound (2p)
Jam	2d a half pound jar (1p)
Milk	1d a pint (½p)
Large loaf	3d (1p)
Tea	4d a quarter pound (2p)

When food ran out, neighbours helped each other:

A middle-class kitchen with dresser and range (1910)

> 'Neighbours would borrow a cup of sugar, a little drop of vinegar, a
> bit of tea, a cup of milk, and if they had any aunts or uncles coming
> on Sunday, a lend of a white table cloth.'
>
> Bristol WEA, *Bristol as We Remember It*

In order to pay for clothes and shoes for the children, many women paid a
couple of pence a week into a clothing club.

Budgets were tight, and when a wife was away, her husband would often
realise how tricky it was to manage. One man looked after his five children
for two weeks while his wife was away:

> 'He apologised for not making the money go as far as "mother" did,
> for buying loaves and not baking the bread, for scrubbing without
> soap, which he had forgotten to buy. The enormous consumption of
> margarine – 3s 6d [17½p] as against 1s 6d [7½p] – is an instance
> of the way in which the father is kept in ignorance of the privations
> which are undergone by his family. Directly he was left in charge,
> this father allowed margarine all round on the same scale as he had
> always used himself, with the result of more than doubling the
> amount spent on it.'
>
> Maud Pember Reeves, *Round About a Pound a Week*

A HOUSEWIFE'S DAY

A day in the life of a working-class housewife about eighty years ago. She
lived in London in two rooms and had six children:

6.00	Nurses baby (feeds it).
6.30	Gets up, calls five children, puts kettle on, washes necks and backs of all children, dresses them and does the girls' hair.
7.30	Gets husband's breakfast, cooks bloater, cuts slices of bread and dripping for children.
8.00	Gives husband breakfast and makes tea.
8.30	He goes, gives children breakfast, sends them to school, has own.
9.00	Clears away and washes up.
9.30	Carries down slops and carries up water from yard. Makes beds.
10.00	Washes and dresses baby, nurses him and puts him to bed.
11.00	Sweeps bedroom, scrubs down stairs and passage.
12.00	Goes out and buys food for the day.
12.30	Cooks dinner, lays table.
1.00	Gives children dinner and nurses baby.
1.45	Washes hands and faces of children and sees them off to school.
2.00	Washes up dinner things, scrubs out kitchen, cleans grate, empties dirty water, fetches more from the yard.
3.00	Nurses baby.
3.30	Cleans herself and begins to mend clothes.
4.15	Children all back.
4.30	Gives them tea.
5.00	Clears away and washes up, nurses the baby and mends clothes.
6.00	Cooks husband's tea.
7.00	Gives husband his tea.
7.30	Puts younger children to bed.
8.00	Tidies up, washes husband's tea things, sweeps kitchen, mends clothes, nurses baby, puts older children to bed.
8.45	Gets husband's supper; mends clothes.
10.00	Nurses baby and makes him comfortable for the night.
10.30	Goes to bed.

Maud Pember Reeves, *Round About a Pound a Week*

THE MISTRESS OF THE HOUSE

'It will be found an excellent plan to write down the daily work of each servant and the hours for doing it as well as the days on which extra cleaning has to be done. The hours for rising, meals, and retiring affect the comfort of the household so much that they also should be written down. The kitchen and larder should be visited daily by the mistress and great comfort will be found in the regular system of writing "bills of fare", they not only ensure that the dinners ordered are served but they act as a check to tradesmen's books.'

Kensington Society, 1892

Women in the upper and well-off middle classes also had responsibility for the home but this meant supervising the work of servants. Mrs Beeton wrote her *Book of Household Management* in 1861 and its popularity for years afterwards suggests that women welcomed advice. She covered all aspects of household management from coping with servants to entertaining, but, most important, she stressed the crucial role of the mistress:

'As with the commander of an Army, or the leader of any enterprise, so is it with the mistress of the house. Her spirit will be seen throughout the whole establishment . . . the highest rank of feminine character is knowledge of household duties.'

Mrs Beeton, *Book of Household Management*

One important task was planning all the meals, although the shopping, cooking, serving and washing up were all done by servants. Mrs Beeton suggested the following list of menus as 'plain family dinners' for a week. And dinner was only one of the three meals at the very least (including a cooked breakfast and cooked supper) that the family would eat:

" PLAIN FAMILY DINNER "

PLAIN FAMILY DINNERS	
Sunday	Codfish and oyster sauce, potatoes Roast mutton, broccoli and potatoes Redcurrant jelly
Monday	Remains of codfish Curried rabbit Dumplings and wine sauce
Tuesday	Boiled fowls, parsley and butter Bacon, sprouts and minced mutton Baroness pudding
Wednesday	Rest of fowl Roast pork and apple, turnips and potatoes Lemon pudding
Thursday	Cold pork Jugged hare, potatoes Apple pudding
Friday	Boiled beef, carrots, turnips, dumplings, potatoes Rice snowballs
Saturday	Pea soup Cold beef and mash Baked batter fruit pudding

Mrs Beeton, *Book of Household Management*

When Margaret Powell left home to become a servant she was shocked at the amount of food that was delivered to her new 'home'.

'The amount of food that came into that house seemed absolutely fabulous to me, the amount of food that was eaten and wasted too . . . when I used to think of my family at home where we seldom had enough to eat it used to break my heart . . . the milkman called three times a day. I've never seen so much milk, cream and eggs. Pints of cream every day were nothing in that household, even when they weren't entertaining.'

Margaret Powell, *Below Stairs*

SERVANTS' DUTIES

In a large and well-to-do home there were men and women servants with their own special jobs. These are the duties of a footman and a housemaid in the 1880s:

'Footmen: The daily round of footmen's duties may be taken as follows:

To rise at half-past six in the summer and seven in the winter; take coals to the sitting-room; clean the boots, trim the lamps, clean the plate; lay the breakfast table for the family; carry in the breakfast; wait at breakfast; remove the breakfast things; answer the door in the morning after 12 o'clock, take out notes if required; lay the luncheon table, take in the luncheon, wait at table, clear the table; wash the silver and glass used at luncheon; lay the dinner-table; go out with the carriage in the afternoon; answer the door to visitors; close the shutters in the sitting-room, attend to the fires therein throughout the day and evening; prepare and assist in carrying in the 5 o'clock tea, clear the table after tea, wash and put away the china; wait at dinner; clear the dinner-table, assist in putting away the plate, wash the glass and silver used at dinner and dessert; prepare and assist in carrying in the coffee to the dining-room; be in attendance in the front hall when dinner guests are leaving the house; attend to the requirements of the gentlemen in the smoking-room; attend to the lighting of the house, as soon as it is dusk, whether lighted with gas, lamps, or candles; clean, arrange, and have in readiness the flat silver candlesticks, before the dressing-bell rings in winter, and by 10 o'clock in summer; go out with the carriage when it is ordered in the evening; valet the young gentlemen of the family. Footmen are usually allowed two suits of livery a year.

Housemaid: The usual duties of a housemaid consist of:

To rise at six in summer and half-past six in winter; before breakfast to sweep and dust the drawing-room, dining-room, front hall, and other sitting-rooms; to clean the grates and light the fires; and where a lady's-maid or valet is not kept, she carries up the water for the baths for the family. After her own breakfast she makes the servants' beds, sweeps, dusts, and arranges the rooms, sweeps the front staircase and front hall.

She makes the best beds, and sweeps and dusts the rooms; cleans the grates, and lights the fires; when fires are kept up in the bed-rooms during the day, it is her duty to attend to them, and to light them morning and evening, or when required; she prepares the bedrooms for the night, turns down the beds, fills the jugs with water, closes the curtains, takes up a can of hot water for each person.

After the family have gone down to dinner, she again makes the round of the bedrooms, and puts them in order; her last duty being to take up a can of hot water to each bedroom and dressing-room.

It is her duty to see, during the day, that each bedroom is supplied with soap, candles, clean towels, writing-paper, and all that is required for use.'

'The Servants' Practical Guide', in E. Royston Pike, *Human Documents of the Age of the Forsytes*

There were also servants to look after the personal needs of the master and mistress of the house, to get their clothes ready for them, help them get ready to go out, deliver messages and organise their social lives for them.

Servants became less common after the 1914–18 war, when women got the chance to do better paid work in factories, with greater independence. Even though they lost these jobs when the men returned after the war, they were not prepared to go back into service. At the same time machines gradually replaced servants in the homes of those who could afford them, and now are found in the majority of homes.

THE MACHINE AGE

The first machines were way beyond the means of most people. In 1906 a vacuum cleaner cost £35 – the same number of weeks wages for working people. A fridge was 24 guineas (£25–4s) in 1939, which doesn't sound a lot but at that time £3 a week was a very good wage. Early machines were often extremely clumsy and heavy; the first electric iron in 1894 weighed 14 lbs. The first vacuum cleaners were huge machines, too large to be used inside

" A HANDY MACHINE FOR THE HOUSEMAID "

165

the house. They were hired and arrived in a cart. Pipes and nozzles were then pushed through the windows of the house — hardly a handy machine for the housemaid.

Most homes weren't supplied with electricity until the 1940s. In 1921 only 12 per cent of homes had electricity; while in 1981, 99 per cent have it. It's only since the 1950s that the electrical goods we rely on so much today have become widely available.

	1948	1963	1980
homes with vacuum cleaners	40%	72%	94%
homes with washing machines	4%	50%	75%
homes with fridges	2%	33%	91%

Other technical changes have affected work in the kitchen, such as the use of aluminium for saucepans and kettles instead of heavy iron. Stainless steel is used for draining boards and cutlery, and plastics provide easy to clean surfaces. Plastic bowls and buckets are lighter than the old enamel ones and do not chip or rust. Beds, chairs and tables are made of lighter materials and gas, electric or oil heating has replaced the coal fire in more and more homes.

AN EASIER LIFE?

In theory, labour-saving machines have made housework much easier. Certainly housework today is a great deal easier, but machines do also encourage high standards in the home. In 1930 the *Ladies' Home Journal* commented:

'Because we housewives today have the tools to reach it, we dig every day after the dust that grandma left . . . If few of us have nine children for a weekly bath, we have two or three for a daily immersion. If our consciences don't prick us over vacant pie shelves or cookie jars, they do over meals in which a vitamin may be omitted or a calorie lacking.'

This was written in America where machines came earlier than in Britain, but perhaps some of these points apply in this country today. It doesn't take all of Monday to do the washing, but several small washes a week may be necessary because the family expect clean clothes every day. A living room that was once cleaned weekly may now get hoovered daily. Freezers and blenders are an encouragement to do more and better cooking. In other words, there are new pressures on the housewife.

Another recent development is high-powered advertising aimed at housewives to encourage them to buy certain products by playing on their conscience: Is your wash white enough? Is your family getting the best food? Should they eat butter or margarine? Are you getting the best value for money?

Many people brought up eighty or a hundred years ago recognise that things have changed, but not always for the best. Mrs Halls, a London woman, explains:

> 'We were more contented then . . . we had nothing and everyone else had nothing . . . now we are all on each other's backs. Our spirit is gone . . . Then if you didn't see the woman next door you knocked on her door . . . now she could die.'
>
> 'I wouldn't want to go back to all that housework, but we are no happier . . . a modern house doesn't make you happy or contented. We got as much pleasure out of going shopping with a few bob as out of anything we've got today.'

There is probably more isolation now that the extended family, where several generations might be in the same house or street, has more or less gone. One area of possible change is sharing housework. More men today help with the chores, cooking and shopping, partly because more married women go out to work than ever before. On the other hand, in the majority of cases it is still the woman who has overall responsibility and does most of the housework. She often takes a job that fits in with home responsibilities, or organises housework and shopping around her job. Most working wives today have two jobs to do, as this recent magazine interview with a newly-wed illustrates:

> 'Chris says she is enjoying being a working wife though it does need organisation. "I find by the time I get home after work and have cooked a meal there's not much of the evening left," she said ruefully. "I've noticed how much more washing there is too. At home I did my own, but now there are my things and Mario's and the sheets and towels too. Our linen basket always seems to be full. Mario takes his turn at cleaning and making the beds which is a help – and I'm sure we'll work out a proper routine over the next few months." '

> *Look Now*, December 1980

QUESTIONS
The house p. 142:
1. How does the furniture differ from what would be bought today? Which items are out of date? Which modern ones are missing?

No mod cons p. 145 and Gas lights and coal fires p. 146:
2. From the evidence here, how was it inconvenient not to have running water, electricity and modern heating in the home?

Cleaning p. 146:
3. From the extracts quoted, in what ways was cleaning harder work a hundred years ago?

Cleanliness is next to godliness p. 147:
4. Do you think some housework was done to impress the neighbours, from the information here? Is housework today ever done to impress neighbours or visitors?

5. How important was money for keeping the house clean? Is it important today?

Washing up p. 149:
6. Washing up was Margaret Powell's 'pet hate'. Why was it such hard work? What do you think is the worst job when it comes to housework?

Washing and ironing p. 149:
7. How long is spent each week in your home doing washing and ironing? Who does it?

Cooking p. 152:
8. What were the difficulties of cooking in a poor home? Does cooking take more or less time and effort today compared with a hundred years ago?

9. In one village, described on page 153, baking was done communally by the women. Which chores can be done communally today?

10. Think of a typical menu for a family with three children today for a week, and compare it with the one given. What are the main differences in the amount and types of food eaten? Why do you think 'extras for him' were included at tea time? Would you expect to find 'extras for him' in most homes today?

Shopping p. 156:
11. Why did most working people have to shop so often? How often is your household shopping done today?

12. Is credit as necessary for most people today as it was a hundred years ago? What is the main form of credit used today?

13. In what ways was shopping different a hundred years ago? Why has it changed?

Managing p. 159:

14.   Which items on the budget from the 1900s would you not buy today? What would you buy that is not included here? What do you think have been the most important changes in our eating habits?

15.   Why did the husband manage the budget less economically than his wife? Do you think this would be the case today?

16.   How was the housewife's day then different from what you would expect today? Do you think it's harder or easier to be a housewife now?

The mistress of the house p. 162

17.   From the description here, how has the job of a comfortably-off housewife changed? Who has servants today?

18.   Would you describe the meals listed here as 'plain family dinners' by today's standards? How do they compare with what you eat today?

Servants' duties p. 164:

19.   What are the main differences between the footman's and the house-maid's responsibilities? Who, in your opinion, had the harder job?

The machine age p. 165:

20.   If a housewife or a housemaid of the 1880s were to work in a home of the 1980s, what changes do you think would strike her most?

An easier life? p. 166:

21.   Why do you think older people have suggested that people were just as happy without the conveniences of modern homes?

22.   From your own experience, and from that of families you know, do you think housework is more equally shared by men and women today than it was a hundred years ago? Do you think it should be shared, and if so, how?

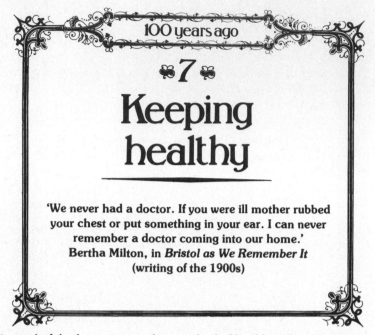

❧7❧
Keeping healthy

'We never had a doctor. If you were ill mother rubbed your chest or put something in your ear. I can never remember a doctor coming into our home.'
**Bertha Milton, in *Bristol as We Remember It*
(writing of the 1900s)**

At the end of the last century, the standard of health in this country was far below that of today. In the 1880s, of the population as a whole:

> **3 out of 4 people died under the age of 40
> 1 out of 2 people died under the age of 20
> 1 in every 4 babies died in its first year**

In the 1980s, the average life expectancy is 73 years. 1 in every 60 babies dies in its first year.

There were huge differences between the health of working-class people and the better-off. The high death-rate of the 1880s was due partly to the unhealthy conditions in which working people lived, as this extract illustrates:

'Houseflies and bluebottles swarmed every kitchen alive: sticky foul-smelling paper traps dangled about, dark with their writhing bodies. And the bed bugs! With the warm days they appeared in battalions, first in the hovels, then in the better class houses, where people waged campaigns against their sickening sweet-odoured presence. Through summer days one saw the "fever van" carrying off some child, who only too often would be seen no more.'
Robert Roberts, *The Classic Slum*

Much of the medical knowledge we have today did not yet exist. The discovery that germs cause certain diseases had not been made; there was no cure for tuberculosis, no penicillin or other antibiotics, no x-rays. There was no health service and people had to pay to see a doctor. Most health care among working people was done by women, who dosed children, nursed husbands, cared for the elderly, and passed on to each other tried and tested cures and remedies.

BABY DEATHS

'When a new baby arrived we would hear people ask "Has it come to stay?" '

Grace Foakes, *Between High Walls*

Babies in working-class families were particularly at risk, not only because of the unhealthy environment but also due to the poor state of their mothers' health. Undernourished women gave birth to sickly babies. They were often unable to breast-feed them. Others could not breast-feed because they had to go out to work:

'I never knew so many bottle-fed babies as there is now. Nearly all the young married women cannot give breast. How is it? . . . Some will not begin with their own milk because they know they have to go out to work.'

Margaret Llewelyn Davies (ed) *Maternity*

The most popular baby food, because it was cheap, was skimmed condensed milk. The labels on the tins showed bonny bouncing babies; in fact this milk lacks the fat content that babies require and today it is marked 'Not suitable for babies'. Many babies developed weak bones and deformed bodies as a result of drinking tinned milk.

An alternative food, similarly cheap, was mashed-up flour and water. The first baby foods which came on to the market in the 1880s were also based on flour, but because flour is very hard for babies to digest, many died from stomach disorders.

Sterilisation was not understood, and bottle-feeding meant the added risk of infection from a germ-ridden bottle. On the following page you will find some advice given to mothers at one of the first clinics opened at the turn of the century. Notice the long tube used for getting the milk from the old-fashioned long-necked bottle.

Because they were believed to have weak backs, babies often had a stiff bandage or binder wound around them very tightly for the first couple of months of life. This restricted their movement and growth, and when this was combined with a poor diet, it meant that many babies became weak and puny and were unlikely to survive if they caught an infection. When they

were ill or teething, babies were given mixtures like 'Godfrey's Cordial', which were bought at the chemist. They sometimes contained dangerous and addictive drugs like opium and many children died from a slight overdose or poisoning. It was simply not realised at the time that these were dangerous, and people used them like we use aspirin today.

CHILDISH AILMENTS

It was when the first State schools were opened in the 1870s that the poor health of working-class children was first recognised. One school visitor described a class of 'scholarship' girls in the 1890s. These were from better-off working-class families − not even from the poorest:

> 'Six of these girls were verminous and seen many times before rejection. Another had very high myopia [short sightedness] . . . one had nasal disease which made her so offensive that she was unfit for attendance. One had advanced valvular disease of the heart. One had only one eye and that of exceedingly defective vision. One was frequently suffering from throat troubles due to enlarged tonsils.'

Midwives visiting a young mother (1890s)

Epidemics at school were common and in some cases fatal. In 1880 these were the illnesses causing most child-deaths: tuberculosis, diphtheria, scarlet fever, smallpox, measles, whooping cough, enteric fever (diarrhoea).

This extract from a school log book records a scarlet fever epidemic:

'16 November – a few scholars absent with scarlatina. Warned all the scholars that if any of their brothers or sisters were taken with scarlatina they were not to come to school.

20 December – attendance still very low in consequence of illness. Walter Smallbones – scholar in third class – died and was buried Christmas week.

1 February – C. Saunders in Infant school died of scarlatina.'

Most people lost a schoolmate at some time, and often a brother or sister. Children from working-class families were far less healthy than those brought up on good food, with decent clothing and housing. In the 1880s the average public schoolboy was five inches taller than a Board schoolboy. In the 1892 measles epidemic it was found that, in working-class Clerkenwell, 91 in every 1000 children died: in middle-class Hampstead, only 52 in every 1000 died. The Medical Officer of Health reported: 'It is only largely fatal to the children of the working classes.'

Children's poor state of health was linked partly to their diet. The importance of vitamins had not yet been discovered and lack of vitamin A in the diet often led to rickets which caused bent backs and bandy legs due to poor bone development. They also lacked medical attention. Teeth were neglected too. A medical officer reported in 1905: 'Among 1000 children I found two who use a toothbrush. A few older children take credit for using one on Sundays.' Some teachers ran toothbrush clubs — 2¼d (1p) for a brush and a good mark in the register if you remembered to use it. Many children — and probably many adults too — preferred toothache to a visit to the dentist because anaesthetics were not used:

> 'I remember myself having two teeth pulled out. One of my older brothers came with me to the dental hospital and when the man in the long white coat asked which one it was to have the teeth pulled out I said very meekly "Me sir". He then looked at my brother and said "What have you come up here for — to 'oller [shout] for him?" Well he pulled them out (and no freezing).'
>
> Albert Paul, *Poverty, Hardship but Happiness*

GIRLS AND BOYS

School health inspections, which were introduced at the end of the century, revealed some differences between the health of boys and girls. It was commoner for girls to have bad eyes because they did sewing in poor light. They were more often anaemic because they had little iron in their diets, and had bad backs from carrying their younger brothers and sisters around. They also had more of a problem with head lice because they had long hair. School medical authorities dealt severely with infected girls. They were sent to a cleansing station where all their hair was cut off; afterwards they had to face their classmates wearing a skullcap. One mother wrote to the teacher:

> 'I should like to know how much more spite you intend to put upon my child — for it is nothing else. First you send the Sanitary Inspector and I have my home taken away . . . and now you cut the few hairs my girl was just beginning to get so nice . . . I know she has no need to have her hair off as it was washed with soft soap last night.'

A school medical examination (1911)

Another wrote:

> 'Please Miss B . . . if the nurse looks at Agnes' head she will find that
> it is quite alright. There might be one or two nits [the eggs] but I
> think she will find they are dead. Her father is not half going on
> about it as he has seen me doing her hair dinner times, tea times and
> at night.'

THE BREADWINNER

Where the man is the main breadwinner his health is vital for the whole
family's survival. A hundred years ago, if he fell ill it meant no wages, and
there was no sick pay or social security. Often wives and children went without food even at better times, so that the breadwinner at least was fed:

> 'If there's anything extra to buy such as a pair of boots for one of the
> children, me and the children goes without dinner — or mebbe only
> 'as a cuppa tea and a bit of bread, but Jim 'ollers to take his dinner to
> work and I give it 'im as usual. He never knows we go without and I
> never tells 'im.'
>
> **Seebohm Rowntree, *Poverty: A Study in Town Life***

Often too the man got the only protein available:

> 'What luxuries people bought at a corner shop often only featured in
> the father's diet and his alone . . . brawn, corned beef, cheese,
> bacon (as little as two ounces of all these). These were the protein

foods vital to sustain a man arriving home at night, worked often to near exhaustion.'

Robert Roberts, The Classic Slum

But although the man might get the lion's share of the food it was hardly enough to keep even him in good health.

NEGLECTING YOURSELF

Wives often neglected their own health for the sake of the rest of the family. They skimped their meals, or went without. Some even starved to death:

> 'An inquest was held touching the death of Catherine Crawley aged thirty years. The deceased was the widow of a mechanic and her husband had been dead five years. The whole family (five children) never took meat more than once in six months. Witness believed she had died from want of food. Dr Bingess said that the verdict was death from starvation.'

Beehive Newspaper, 1871

Many women suffered from internal complaints, especially after having

Bleach packers with flannel face masks, Gateshead (1870s)

children, but they had neither the time nor the money to do anything about it:

> 'I had inflammation of the bladder and of the kidneys besides other complications . . . like the majority of women I thought it was one of the ills I had to bear.'
>
> Margaret Llewelyn Davies (ed) *Maternity*

HAZARDS OF WORK

Many men and women suffered from health problems because of the dreadful conditions under which they worked. The trade union movement was still in its early stages, and health and safety regulations such as we have today did not exist. Most industrial jobs were damaging to health in some way. A baker's job is not a particularly dangerous one, but in the 1880s bakers worked in very unhealthy conditions as this report shows:

> 'He works for long hours in an almost tropical temperature and inhales the gas laden air of a bakehouse, often small and ill-ventilated, and very generally placed below the level of the ground. The average hours in London are 70–80 per week but some are employed for 90 or even 100 hours. Behind the floury whiteness of their workaday face lies too often the pallor of ill health.'
>
> Charles Booth, *Life and Labour of the London Poor*

Bleach powder packers, with inadequate protective clothing, suffered from 'gassing':

> 'The duties of the powder packer consist of filling casks with bleaching powder. To do that he has to enter the chamber, which for several days has been filled with chlorine gas. Though the worst of this gas has been allowed to pass out of the chamber before the packer enters it, the atmosphere is still charged with the deadly fumes. The heat is sometimes tremendous, especially as the poor wretch who has to endure it is swathed about the head in a way that would protect him from Arctic cold.
>
> "What is it like being gassed?" I asked a man. "Like having a hot poker shoved down your throat," was the answer. "You feel done for . . . whether you lie by a day or longer, it takes you fully a week to get over it. Sometimes your mate will help you with your share and you stay about and make a show of helping but it is no good. When the stuff has got down your throat you can't eat anything. If you manage to swallow you vomit it up again directly."
>
> Gassing is such a common matter that the men would describe its symptoms as they would tell you what their Sunday dinner was like.'
>
> *Home Office Report*, 1893

Women and men worked in unhealthy conditions in factories. Marie Paterson, a trade union leader, described conditions for women in a jam factory:

> 'Young girls, thinly clad, thin and pale, and as you stand and talk to them the condensed steam drops down on you and them from the roof so that you are not surprised that the thin cotton dresses they wear are saturated and even their hair is dripping wet. In the resigned manner that is characteristic of this class of worker they admit that "it's a bit steamy".'

These girls suffered from bronchitis, chest diseases and lumbago as a result of their work.

Matchmaking was another job that was very damaging to the health of those who did it — mostly young women. They suffered from 'phossy jaw' a serious jaw disease, which they got from bending over beds of phosphorous, and chest and throat complaints from working with sulphur.

HOME CURES

Every mother had her 'home cures', often handed down through generations, and in many streets there was a local woman, to whom everyone went for medical advice.

A well-known cure for whooping cough was to go down to the gasworks and inhale the fumes. Coughs and colds were a constant problem in winter for those in damp, unheated houses, and cough mixtures were home-made, mostly based on onions and vinegar. One way believed to prevent colds was to sew children into brown paper vests smeared with thick lard. They then kept them on all winter. An investigation among London school children in the 1870s found that by the end of the winter, one in three hadn't taken off their clothes for six months.

Many medicines were made from herbs, either grown in the garden or bought from the local herbalist. There were other cheap and easily obtainable ingredients. Here are some common home-made recipes:

```
saffron – for measles
elderflower and home-made lard – for sores
grated acorns – for diarrhoea
heated onion – for earache
cobwebs – to stop bleeding
```

Some were a little outlandish, like the East Anglian cure for whooping cough — eating a fried field mouse!

There was a strong belief that 'prevention was better than cure', and every

A chemist's (1890s)

week children were dosed with castor oil, Epsom salts or even soap and water to keep them regular. Another belief was that rhubarb taken regularly would 'clear the blood'.

By the end of the century, there were a number of pills and tonics available from chemists – for example, 'Holloway's Pills' which claimed to cure all kinds of ailments.

In fact a legal case brought against Dr Holloway revealed that the pills contained 'butter, lard, turps, wax and nothing else'.

COMMUNITY CARE

In working-class districts, there was a great deal of mutual help among neighbours during illness. For example, it was common practice to spread straw on the road to reduce the noise of horses and carts if someone in the street was ill, and door knockers were muffled.

> 'There was a marvellous neighbourly spirit in those days. If you were ill, the whole street was concerned and wanted to do something about it and they did. They took it in turns to make milk puddings and custards out of their little money. Anything they could do to help.'
>
> John Langley, *Always a Layman*

179.

Women made sure that anyone who was sick was visited:

> 'How many times, I wonder, have I been sent by my aunt up the street to some neighbour; "Take this bowl of soup to Mrs Beasley and ask her if she feels any better. Oh and ask her if you can get her any errands while you're there. Don't drop the basin." '
>
> Arthur Newton, *Years of Change*

If a woman had a baby, neighbours would do the washing and feed the other children until she was on her feet again . . . Sometimes there was a 'neighbourhood box' which was loaned to any woman who needed it when she had her baby. Mrs Bartholomew's mother made a lot of such items. 'They would have sheets, pillowcases, nightdresses for the woman and little clothes for the baby. It helped them over that month you see.' (Interviewed by Anna Davin, 1973.)

Any woman who was particularly skilled or knowledgeable was happy to be consulted:

> 'I lived in Salisbury Street. It was a street of good neighbours. I well remember one lady, Granny Hedges; she was the street doctor. Any young mother who had an illness, especially with children, she could tell what was wrong and could give them free advice.'
>
> Sid Stephens in *Bristol as We Remember It*

The local shop might play the role of today's doctor's surgery:

> 'They used to come to me with all their ailments: "Look at those spots"; they wouldn't dream of going to Boots. "Tell me if I've got to go to the doctor." We used to have a lot of people come in with burns, and I used to say "Come in tomorrow and I'll re-dress it. I became a semi-doctor." '
>
> Neil Griffiths, *Shops Book Brighton 1900–30*

THE HANDYWOMAN

Most babies were born at home, which was then far safer than going into hospital. One in 29 hospital births ended in the mother's death in the 1880s, compared with one in 212 home births.

Usually the birth was attended by the local 'handywoman', who was an experienced but untrained midwife. One such midwife described her work:

> 'I read and asked questions of the doctors and in this way knew a great deal of the theory of midwifery and I was gaining experience in the practical part. The doctors left so much to me and did so little for their fee, that people asked me to take their cases without a doctor.'
>
> Mrs Layton 'Memories of Seventy Years',
> in Margaret Llewelyn Davies (ed) *Life as We Have Known It*

Mrs Shaw worked as a midwife too, although she had the official training which was introduced in 1902:

> 'When I became a midwife there were no drugs. Some midwives gave them gin. The woman had a lot more pain then. You gave them a list of the things you needed – a big new saucepan to boil things up in and you took what you needed and did the best you could. I remember one man who bathed all the kids while his wife gave birth. Then after the delivery he brought her a cup of tea and a jam tart . . . he was exceptional! Mostly it was up to the women neighbours to help.'

The doctor was only called if there were complications. His fee was £1 10/– (£1.50p), whereas even a qualified midwife charged only 3/– (15p). Also doctors were often less sympathetic and more clumsy:

> 'I had a very long illness through the doctor hurrying the birth instead of giving nature a chance, and he was rough in handling me. The result was a three month illness.'
>
> Margaret Llewelyn Davies (ed) *Maternity*

In the 1880s, 15 out of every 3000 mothers died giving birth.
In the 1980s, 15 out of every 100,000 die.

The most common cause of death in childbirth was 'puerperal' or 'child-bed' fever. Often this was caused by the doctor carrying germs from other infected patients:

> 'The third day I developed child-bed fever. I went blind, sometimes unconscious. I was almost beyond hope and seriously ill for three weeks.'
>
> Margaret Llewelyn Davies (ed) *Maternity*

DOCTORS

Because he was expensive poor people only called the doctor in a real emergency, and often fear of going to the doctor was greater than fear of the illness. Since doctors could make a very good living in wealthy neighbourhoods, it was often the least experienced or worst doctors who worked in working-class districts. Even so, they were looked up to and treated with respect, as Mr Churcher remembered of the 1900s:

> 'They all had the same routine: silk hat, walking cane, white gloves and a Gladstone bag in which they had their stethoscope and other

"DOCTORS ALL HAD THE SAME ROUTINE : SILK HAT, WALKING CANE, WHITE GLOVES AND A GLADSTONE BAG."

items. The usual formula when my father was ill was that the doctor would be shown into the parlour, the best room of the house, and the first thing he would do would be to take one glove off, then the other glove off, put them both on the table, then put the walking stick on the table, then the top-hat, and then go upstairs to see the patient. After that he'd come down and have a talk with the wife or whoever it was, don his gloves slowly and methodically, get his walking stick, put on his hat and say "Good Morning!" '

Mr Churcher, The Threepenny Doctor

For those who couldn't afford a home visit, there were clinics or dispensaries where for a few pence you could get a brief examination and a bottle of medicine. Albert Cullington remembers:

'There were rows and rows of forms [benches] and you would gradually shift up and shift up 'til eventually, after a long wait, it was your turn and then you went in. The doctor of course would only spend a minute or so with you as each one had so many to deal with.'

Albert Collington, The Threepenny Doctor

It might also mean a very long walk there and back for the patient, as these places were few and far between. This could easily make people feel worse:

'Outdoor patients have to wait hours with babies on their arms that ought to be in warm rooms and not subjected to the fatigue of being brought through the streets.'

Medical Journal, 1877

HOSPITALS

A hundred years ago, if a person was taken ill suddenly, there was no ambulance service to get him or her to hospital. Most hospitals were privately run, so you had to get a 'hospital letter' before they would take you in. This was a letter of recommendation from one of the wealthy people who donated money to the hospital. Asking for a letter could be humiliating, as George Moore described in his novel *Esther Waters*, written in the 1890s. Esther was pregnant and unmarried, which made matters worse:

> ' "You've got a letter?"
> "No."
> "Then you must get a letter from one of the subscribers."
> "But I don't know any."
> "You can have a book of their names and addresses."
> "But I know no one."
> "You needn't know them. You can go and call. Take those that live nearest – that's the way it is done."
> . . . In Cumberland Place she was received by an elderly lady who said she did not wish to judge anyone, but it was her invariable practice to give letters only to married women.
> The next house she called at the lady was not at home, but she was expected back presently, and the maidservant asked her to take a seat in the hall. But when Esther refused information about her troubles she was called a stuck-up thing who deserved all she got, and was told there was no use to her waiting. At the next place she was received by a footman who insisted on her communicating her business to him. Then he said he would see if his master was in. He wasn't in; he must have just gone out.'
>
> George Moore, *Esther Waters*

Many hospitals were very unhygienic places, and there was no guarantee that the patient's illness would be properly treated. By the 1890s, however, largely under the influence of Florence Nightingale's work, standards of hygiene and nursing in hospitals had greatly improved. Nevertheless many people still believed that, in the words of one man, 'you were likely to come out worse than you went in'.

MEETING THE COST

Without a government scheme of health insurance as we have today many people joined 'Friendly Societies' or 'Sickness Clubs' to cover the cost of illness. Often these were organised by trades unions to help their members when they were off work through illness. Most sickness insurance schemes protected the male worker but not his wife or children.

Shelter for homeless men (1880)

Without insurance, the only resort when serious illness struck was the local workhouse. This was also the only place where old people could go if they could not manage to support themselves. They were grim places, and there was a strong sense of shame and disgrace attached to the idea of becoming a 'pauper' and going into the workhouse. This is one person's memory:

> 'Everyone there was dressed in a uniform, the men in thick navy suits and the women in thick navy dresses; you always knew where they lived the moment you saw them – their clothes gave them away. I have known many an old person who struggled to exist on a few shillings a week rather than go there. I don't think they were badly treated. It was the indignity of it that was so hard to bear, and even people as poor as these had their pride.'
>
> **Grace Foakes,** *Between High Walls*

This is what happened when one couple both fell ill in 1890:

> 'Mr T, Margaret Place, Gascoigne Place, Bethnal Green, is a boot-maker by trade. Is a good hand, and has earned 3/6d a day. He was taken ill last Christmas, and went to the London Hospital; was there three months. A week after he had gone, Mrs T had rheumatic fever, and was taken to Bethnal Green Infirmary, where she

remained about three months. Directly after they had been taken ill, their furniture was seized for three weeks' rent which was owing. Consequently, on becoming convalescent, they were homeless . . . He then had 2d, and she had 6d, which a nurse had given her . . . Next day he had a day's work and got 2/6d and on the strength of this they took a furnished room at 10d per day (payable nightly). His work lasted a few weeks, when he was again taken ill, lost his job and spent all their money. Pawned a shirt and apron for 1 shilling; spent that too. At last pawned their tools for 3 shillings, which got them a few days' food and lodging. He is now minus tools and cannot work at his own job, and does anything he can. Spent their last 2d on a pen'orth each of tea and sugar.'

William Booth, *In Darkest England and the Way Out*

DEATH

Another worrying expense was a funeral. The very cheapest burial for a child in the 1890s was £1.10s (£1.50p), and for an adult it would have been considerably more. People who couldn't afford a funeral had a 'pauper's burial', paid for by the local workhouse, without a hired car or an individually marked grave. This was regarded as the worst possible humiliation, and many families saved all their lives with a burial club, paying perhaps 3d a week for father, 2d for mother, and 1d for each child, to ensure a modest but respectable funeral. Even so, one in five people had a pauper's burial in 1900.

This family managed the humblest funeral in the 1900s:

'The three-year-old daughter of a carter out of work died of tuberculosis. The father, whose policies had lapsed, borrowed the sum of £2.5s necessary to bury the child. The mother was four months paying the debt off by reducing the food of herself and of the five other children. The funeral cortège consisted of one vehicle, in which the little coffin went under the driver's seat. The parents and a neighbour sat in the back part of the vehicle. They saw the child buried in a common grave with twelve other coffins of all sizes. "We 'ad to keep a sharp eye out for Edie," they said, "she were so little she were almost 'id." '

Maud Pember Reeves, *Round About a Pound a Week*

Among the better-off working classes — publicans or shopkeepers, for example — a funeral was a grand affair. There was a procession of horse-drawn carriages with black plumes on the horses and over the hearse. Afterwards there was food and drink. The body was kept at home for about a week for friends and neighbours to see. Children were quite used to seeing the dead:

A funeral with 'extras' (late nineteenth century)

> **'When we were kids we used to go and knock at the door and ask if we could go and see the bodies. They used to take us upstairs with a candle.'**
>
> **Thea Vigne, 'Parents and Children 1890–1918'**

Women helped each other when there was a death. They looked after the body, prepared it for burial, and organised the refreshments. Everyone in the street drew their curtains as a sign of respect. Often a 'Friendly Lead' was held in the local pub. This was a sing-song, with a charge for entry, and all the neighbours of the dead person were invited. The money helped the family to pay for the funeral.

ILLNESS AS A LUXURY

The better-off might have been expected to need the services of doctors far less than poor people. Yet at the end of the last century, upper-class women spent a lot of time and money at the doctor's.

This was partly a fashion, much encouraged by doctors, who made a great deal of profit from it. Wealthy women were encouraged to believe that frailty and weakness were feminine and attractive:

> **'I think it is in the increased attention paid to women and especially in their new function as lucrative patients . . . that we find explanation for much of the ill-health among women, freshly discovered today.'**
>
> **Mary Putnam, 1895**

186

Much of the so-called frailty of women and their tendency to faint at the slightest excuse was probably due to the fashion of wearing very tight corsets which not only restricted their breathing but in some cases did permanent damage to their internal organs. Women were told by their doctors that periods were an 'illness' making them incapable of doing anything:

> 'At such times women are unfit for any great mental or physical labour. They suffer under a languor and depression which disqualifies them from thought or action and renders it extremely doubtful how far they can be considered responsible beings while the crisis lasts.'
>
> Dr James MacGregor Allan, 1869

Dr Henry Maudsley wrote in the *Fortnightly Review*:

> 'For one quarter of each month during the best years of her life, woman is more or less sick and unfit for hard work.'

It is worth bearing in mind that any upper-class woman who took to her bed was waited on by a maid who had to work every day of the year regardless of how she felt.

Not all women were content to accept what doctors said:

> 'The actual period of childbirth apart, the ordinary healthy woman is as fit for work every day of her life as the ordinary healthy man.'
>
> Dame Millicent Fawcett, Suffragist

> 'Working class women continue working without intermission and as a rule without ill effects.'
>
> Elizabeth Garrett Anderson, Britain's first woman doctor

A close look at the kind of lives well-off women were expected to lead suggests that being ill might well have been a handy excuse to escape boring social visits, endless evenings sitting at home, and making polite conversation. Florence Nightingale, herself brought up in this kind of world, wrote:

> 'A woman was heard to wish that she could break a limb that she might have a little time to herself.'
>
> Florence Nightingale, *Cassandra*, in Ray Strachey, *The Cause*

She said she often spent the whole evening longing for the hands of the clock to reach ten so that she could go up to her room and be alone.

Hysteria was apparently common among women who could afford to consult their doctors. Probably outbreaks of extreme rage and hysteria were the only outlets for the frustrating and idle lives many women of the upper and middle classes were forced to lead.

Doctors prescribed drastic measures including surgery rather in the same way that today many women who suffer from depression are given drugs because their doctors are unable to do anything to change the conditions that are causing the depression in the first place. Some doctors in the last century believed that the ovaries were the cause of all female illness, and might advise a patient showing signs of stress to have them removed when there was absolutely nothing wrong with them. This in itself was bad enough: but records show that half these operations were fatal.

An alternative to an operation was a 'rest-cure'. The patient was supposed to lie flat in bed and do nothing for weeks. Complete passivity was the idea. One American woman who experienced this treatment described it in her book *The Yellow Wallpaper*, written in 1892. Slowly but surely the patient went mad, creeping around the yellow walls of her room. She eventually realised that the real cure for her would have been involvement in work, useful activity, and companionship:

> 'I think sometimes that if I were only well enough to write a little it would relieve the press of ideas and rest me.
>
> But I find I get pretty tired when I try.
>
> It is so discouraging not to have any advice and companionship about my work. When I get really well, John says we will ask Cousin Henry and Julia down for a long visit; but he says he would as soon put fireworks in my pillow-case as to let me have those stimulating people about now.
>
> I wish I could get well faster.
>
> But I must not think about that. This paper looks at me as if it knew what a vicious influence it had!'
>
> **Charlotte Perkins Gilman**, *The Yellow Wallpaper*

Towards the end of the century, more and more women of the better-off classes were breaking out of the restricted lives they had been expected to lead. Many were campaigning for the right to vote, or to enter the professions, such as medicine. Male doctors fiercely opposed the entry of women into their profession on the grounds that they were unfit to cope with the job. One leading doctor said: 'Women are unfit for the hard and incessant toil . . . they will learn subjects which would be shocking to the female mind.' Possibly this view was sometimes coloured by the fact that if women became qualified doctors themselves, men would lose their most profitable patients.

HEALTH IMPROVEMENTS

To a great extent, bad health among working people a hundred years ago arose from poverty and poor living conditions. In 1899, when large numbers of men volunteered to fight in the Boer War in Africa, 8000 out of the 12,000 volunteers in one town were rejected as unfit; many more were too unhealthy for the doctor even to examine, and only 1200 passed as fit to join the army. This caused great concern in government circles about the health of the male population — the country's fighting force. A state insurance scheme was eventually set up in 1911 for working men; women and children were not included. It was based on contributions from wages, much as National Insurance is today.

At the end of the First World War, in 1918, the government pledged itself to build 'Homes fit for Heroes'. However, only marginal improvements were made. Conditions were still appalling in the 1930s, as this extract, written in 1939, illustrates:

> 'Here is a woman from Rochdale, Mrs J, who has become almost hysterical in her horror of the conditions in which she lives: "There are plenty of drawbacks, over-crowded, dirt back and front, as we have no back-door, damp floors, damp walls, no convenience, walls and floor leaving each other." She suffers from headaches, nerves and bad rheumatism.'
>
> M. Spring-Rice, *Working-Class Wives*, 1939

In 1946, the National Health Service was set up to provide free medical treatment for everyone. The fear of doctors' bills no longer prevents the poor and unemployed from getting medical help, though the charge for prescriptions sometimes does. Medical science and research have brought about a better understanding of the body and how it works, of food values and nutrition, of germs and bacteria. More effective treatment is now available and it is less painful and dangerous than it used to be; doctors and midwives are highly trained and make use of the latest technology.

Yet there is still much that needs to be done. We are far from curing all illnesses. TB can now be cured and has largely disappeared from Britain, but in its place are such illnesses as cancer and heart disease, which cause a high proportion of deaths. Insufficient money is made available by governments for research into such diseases. Some highly technical methods of treating diseases like dialysis machines for kidney failure are expensive and cannot be made available to everyone. Modern life has brought its own health problems, unknown earlier; injury from car crashes, lung cancer from cigarette smoking, mental stress resulting from too fast a pace of living. Now that people live longer, the illnesses of old age are far more common. There are some patients who are in hospital too as a result of drugs and treatment they have been given which have themselves caused further complications. We rely much more on being treated by doctors when we fall ill, but there are still far too few preventative measures to help people avoid ill-health in the first place.

We, in this country, are fortunate in having a relatively high standard of health care compared with much of the rest of the world. Nevertheless lives are still lost, just as they were a hundred years ago, and people still suffer ill-health unnecessarily.

This newspaper report refers to a proposal by the Social Services Committee to reduce the numbers of babies born with handicaps, and therefore requiring special and expensive care:

> 'The report by the Commons Select Committee on Social Services estimated that at least 5000 babies are born with handicaps which could have been prevented. But the Department of Health and Social Security in a White Paper argued that the cost of the recommendations would be ten times the savings . . .
>
> The Committee . . . aimed at reducing baby mortality rates through health education, improved ante-natal care, and better facilities and staffing in hospital maternity units . . .
>
> In the White Paper, Mr Jenkin made it plain that the Government could not spend this sort of money.'
>
> *The Observer*, 28 December 1980

QUESTIONS

Baby deaths p. 171:

1. There were a number of reasons for the high death rate at the turn of the century among young babies. What were they? Why are babies less likely to die in Britain today?

Childish ailments p. 172:

2. Why did so many more children die in Clerkenwell than in Hampstead? What differences would you expect to find between the health of children from different areas today, and why?

Girls and boys p. 174:

3. Why did the mothers who wrote these letters resent the school's interference so much? How much responsibility for children's health do schools have today?

The breadwinner p. 175:

4. Why did the man get better food? Do you think it was sufficient? Do you think it was right that he should get more?

Neglecting yourself p. 176:

5. Why did many women neglect their health? Do you think this still happens today? Do you think there is any truth in the idea sometimes put forward that women are better at putting up with pain and suffering than men? Do you think they should have to bear more pain than men?

190

Hazards of work p. 177:

6.   What exactly made baking, powder packing and matchmaking bad for the health, as described in the three extracts? Which substances cause illness and disease at work today?

Home cures p. 178:

7.   Which of these home remedies do you think might have been most effective? Do you know of any home remedies today?

Community care p. 179:

8.   Would you find similar examples of neighbourly help today? Do you think neighbours did more in those days to help each other when they were ill, or does illness still bring out the best in people?

The handywoman p. 180:

9.   Why do you think most women used the local midwife rather than the doctor? Why have doctors replaced midwives, and hospital births replaced home births? Has this been a change for the better?

Doctors p. 181:

10.   From Mr Churcher's account, why do you think doctors were looked up to by working people? Do you think this attitude still exists?

Hospitals p. 183:

11.   Why do you think Esther was refused hospital letters in three houses? Are there any difficulties in getting into hospital today?

Meeting the cost p. 183:

12.   From William Booth's description on page 184–5, why was illness such a disaster in a working-class family? How does serious illness affect working-class families today?

Death p. 185:

13.   Why do you think a decent funeral was considered to be so important?

14.   What strikes you most about the photograph of a funeral on page 186? Find out how much a funeral costs today. Why is the expense less of a worry than it was a hundred years ago?

Illness as a luxury p. 186:

15.   What reasons did the doctors quoted on page 187 give for claiming that women were not always fit? Why do you think they said this? Why was there no such concern about men's health problems?

16.   Why do you think women were so often described as 'hysterical'? Look up the origin of the word 'hysteria'. Which Greek word is it based on, and why?

Health improvements p. 188:

17.   What do you think has been the development most responsible for better health in this country today? What are the main reasons for ill health in other countries, particularly in the Third World?

18.   Do you think there are any ways in which better health could be encouraged and developed in Britain today?

✤ 8 ✤

In your spare time

'As far as the women are concerned there is still less provision for their recreation than for that of the men, except by private undertaking of one kind or another. As to public places, there are not many in this country where it is the custom for ordinary respectable working women to go.'
Lady Florence Bell, *At the Works*.

A hundred years ago most working people had nothing like the leisure time we have today. Work, both inside and outside the home, took up much more time and most people had less spare cash to spend than they have now. There were fewer ready-made amusements — no radio, television, records, tapes, cinemas or sports centres. There were no cars either — only bicycles, horse-drawn buses and trams or railways.

Of course, people did find all sorts of ways of enjoying what free time they had, and these varied between town and country and different regions. Apart from these variations, there was a great difference between the leisure activities of men and women. Women were far more restricted in where they could go and what they could do.

To some extent this depended on whether or not a woman was married. Single people of both sexes had more money and freedom to go out, but once married, a woman was very much tied to the home. A London health visitor, Mrs Shaw, described the people she knew:

'When the man came home he had his freedom to go out if he wanted; most of them did nothing in the home, wouldn't even wash up. But the women, they never stopped, and they never had an outing further than the back yard.'

THE PUB

At the end of the century, drink was blamed as the chief cause of working-class poverty. In 1885, it was claimed that the average working-class family spent a quarter of their income on drink. In London in 1902 one house in every 77 was reckoned to be a pub. Of course, the wealthier classes drank heavily too, but this wasn't considered the same problem, since they could afford it.

The drunken working-class father who wasted his earnings was regarded by some people as typical. Temperance societies were formed to persuade working men to 'take the pledge' and give up drinking. In fact although there was a lot of heavy drinking among the poor, far more typical was the working man who went to his local pub for a modest pint in the evening. The pub was an all-male institution in many areas, as Flora Thompson described:

> 'Forlow might boast of its church, its school, its annual concert, its quarterly penny reading, but the hamlet did not envy it these amenities, for it had its own social centre, warmer, more human and altogether preferable, in the tap-room of the "Waggon and Horses".
>
> There the adult male population gathered every evening to sip its half pints, drop by drop, to make them last and to discuss local events, wrangling over politics or farming methods or to sing a few songs "to oblige".
>
> It was an innocent gathering. None of them got drunk; they had not money enough; even with beer and good beer at twopence a pint. Yet the parson preached from the pulpit against it, going so far on one occasion to call it a den of iniquity. " 'Tis a great pity he can't come and see what it's like for himself," said one of the older men on

the way home from church. "Pity he can't mind his own business," retorted a younger one.

Only about half a dozen men held aloof from the circle and those were either known to "have religion" or suspected of being "close wi' their ha'pence". The others went as a matter of course, appropriating their own special seats on settle or bench. It was as much their home as their own cottages, and far more homelike than many of them, with its roaring fire, red window curtains and well scoured pewter.

To spend their evenings there was indeed, as the men argued, a saving, for, with no man in the house, the fire at home could be let die down and the rest of the family could go to bed when the room got cold.

It was exclusively a men's gathering. The wives never accompanied them; though sometimes a woman who had got her family off her hands and so had a few pence to spend on herself, would knock at the back door with a bottle or jug and perhaps linger a little, herself, unseen, to listen to what was going on within.'

Flora Thompson, *Lark Rise to Candleford*

Single factory girls who had their own money might have had more opportunity to go out drinking but they often met with considerable disapproval, as this description shows:

'Before holiday times girls save up their money and go into public houses directly they are paid off. Then each girl stands a 2d whisky to her friends and if it is a party of five or six friends each girl has five or six glasses, and pays ten pence or a shilling [4–5p]. Sometimes

"JUST GOING TO TAKE YER 'USBAND DOWN THE PUB MARY, SAVE ON THE HOUSEKEEPING MONEY, EH?"

they go together in even a larger party and spend each one as much as two shillings or two and sixpence [10–12½p]. I asked how they could possibly afford it, when their wages were only ten shillings a week [50p]. "They pay first and afford it afterwards," I was told. "Do the girls do this in your starch factory?" I asked one of the girls' sisters. "No," she answered, "because our forewoman is a member of the Temperance Association and most of the girls are teetotallers." '

Alys Russell, 'Four Days in a Factory', *Contemporary Review, 1903*

It was partly a question of custom. In the East End of London it was quite acceptable for women to go to pubs, as Booth reported in his 1902 survey:

'Go into any of these houses – the ordinary public house at the corner of the ordinary East End street – there, standing at the counter or seated on the benches against the wall or partition will be perhaps a dozen people, men and women, chatting together over their beer, more often beer than spirits. Behind the bar will be a decent middle-aged woman, something above her customers in class, neatly dressed, respecting herself and respected by them.'

Charles Booth, *Life and Labour of the People of London*

The pub was often a centre of entertainment too:

'Once grandfather was boozed he would set up his drums and accompany the piano player singing at the top of his voice until closing time. He would sing songs like "It's a Great Big Shame", "Soldiers of the Queen", and "We All Came Into the World with Nothing". His whole body would tremble with the effort of hitting the top notes . . . then he would become silent, lay down his drumsticks and stand up most solemnly. The mood had changed. Grandfather was now ready to give out with his tear-jerkers; songs like "I'll Take You Home again, Kathleen", "It's Only a Beautiful Picture in a Beautiful Golden Frame".'

Ron Barnes, *Coronation Cups and Jam Jars*

SPENDING MONEY

In the 1890s:

A pint of beer cost	2d (1p)
A bottle of whisky cost	3s 6d (17½p)
10 Weights or Woodbine Cigarettes cost (they could also be bought singly)	2d (1p)
½oz tobacco and papers to roll your own cost	4d (2p)

Most men had their own spending money which they kept out of their wages while their wives were given the rest for housekeeping. In one village for example:

> 'The men's spending money was fixed at a shilling a week [5p], seven pence [3p] for the nightly half pint and the balance for other expenses. An ounce of tobacco was bought for them by their wives with the groceries.'
>
> Flora Thompson, *Lark Rise to Candleford*

In Lambeth, at the turn of the century, it was reported:

> 'He may spend perhaps 2d a day on beer, 1d a day on tobacco, and 2d a day on tram fares, and that without being a monster of selfishness or wishing to deprive his children of their food.'
>
> Maud Pember Reeves, *Round About a Pound a Week*

There are no accounts of wives having their own spending money, even when they were earning. Anything a woman spent on extras she saved out of the housekeeping through her own economies. Working-class women rarely smoked before this century, except elderly women who sometimes smoked clay pipes. A special treat might consist of a night out with her husband, for which the woman had saved up. Out of thirty couples visited in Lambeth at the beginning of this century, two had had one night out over the period of a month, for which the wife had budgeted:

> 'One was a young newly married couple. The visitor smilingly hoped they had enjoyed themselves. " 'E treated me," said the wife proudly! "Then why does it come out of your budget?" asked the visitor. The girl stared. "Oh, I paid," she explained, "he lets me take him." The other case was of two middle-aged people of about thirty where there were four children. Here again the wife paid.'
>
> Maud Pember Reeves, *Round About a Pound a Week*

Only single woman had their own spending money. This is how one woman weaver spent her money in the 1880s:

Wages 13s 6d (67½p)	Board 8s (40p)
	Dress 1s 9d (8p)
	Amusements 1d (½p)
	Holidays & picnics 3½d (1½ – 2p)
	Education 3d (1½p)

A NIGHT OUT

The most popular night out for working-class people was to a music hall or local theatre. This is a description of a music hall audience in Middlesborough:

> 'In the two music halls in the town, which are always full, the dearest places – excepting the boxes, to which apparently only a select public go – are 1s [5p], the price of the orchestra stalls. The dress circle is 6d [2½p], the pit 4d [2p], the gallery 2d [1p]. In the gallery there are always a great number of boys, as well as in the pit. The front row of the gallery generally consists of small children, little boys between seven and ten, eagerly following every detail of the entertainment. Each of them must have paid 2d [1p] for his place.
>
> There are workmen to be seen in the orchestra stalls; this means 1s [5p] a night. If a man takes his wife that means 2s [10p]; but there are more men than women to be seen here. Women go oftener to the cheaper places. One may see a queue of them waiting to go in the 2d [1p] seats often with their husbands accompanying them. Many of these women have their babies in their arms. There is no doubt that they come out looking pleased and brightened up.'
>
> Lady Florence Bell, *At the Works*

A selection of artists performed various acts. This is part of a typical programme:

> 'Harry Champion, with his Cockney dress sang songs – all quick-fire timing, finishing with a little step dance to the tune of "Any Old

A village cricket team (1890s)

Iron". Jack Pleasant's "The Lancashire Lad" complete with button-
hole flower and simple patter made us laugh. George Jackley and in
later years Nat Jackley's the guardsman dance, complete with
busby, had to be seen to be believed.'

John Blake, *Memories of Old Poplar*

For many couples the Saturday night outing was going to the market for
bargains. According to this writer, the women seemed to do most of the
work:

'Men, women and children all good-humoured and well dressed, out
for marketing and to see the fun or for the promenade simply; and all
young. In the market itself there was great seriousness. Most were
coming away with their purchases in large paper parcels, but a good
number were still buying and the market place was full. The man
never carried the parcels, except where the woman had a child in
her arms, and not always then.'

Charles Booth, *Life and Labour of the London Poor*

SPORT AND GAMBLING

Among working-class people, only men played sport. Some went to watch
football on Saturday afternoons if they got a free half day, or to play for a
local team. Boxing, whippet racing and pigeon fancying were popular in
some areas.

Betting was popular, too. There were no legal betting shops like today, so
when bets were arranged at work, someone had to run round to the book-
maker's house with the bet. In Middlesborough, for example:

'The most prevalent form of gambling is betting on horse racing.
Besides this, the men bet on billiards, on cards, on dominoes, on
football matches. Betting on races is made fatally easy for them by
the elaborate organisation of the tipsters for supplying information
and facilities and by the extraordinary amount that is written about
it in the papers.'

Lady Florence Bell, *At the Works*

While women couldn't get away from the house for sports meetings, they
could easily have a bet because bookmakers went round from door to door:

'The systematic betting of the women, encouraged by bookmakers,
is in many cases a deliberate effort, with or without the knowledge of
the husband, to add to the income. A man comes to the door of a
woman who either from her own thriftlessness or from stern neces-
sity is hard pressed for money, and presents her with the possibility
of spending a shilling and winning £5. How should she not listen to

Street corner, Hackney (1886)

him? She takes the bet, and it may actually happen that she wins; and if she does, small possibility that any subsequent arguments or exhortations against the practice should have any effect.'

Lady Florence Bell, *At the Works*

ON THE STREETS

For unmarried working people the centre of social life was the local street — the only place where they could get away from parents and younger brothers and sisters. In Salford the young men gathered on the street corners and hung around in groups:

'Generally, all boys after a few weeks' work were eligible for these gatherings, though upper-class parents frowned on their sons entering except perhaps to join in football games. Schoolboys, girls, women and married men kept their distance, the last of course, having their own rendezvous socially much superior in the tavern.'

Robert Roberts, *The Classic Slum*

Single women didn't hang around the streets so much but they did go walking in groups. This writer is describing London:

> 'The love which these young people have for the streets is wonderful, especially this is the case with the girls. When they leave their social club at ten they go back every night to the streets and walk about 'til midnight!'
>
> Walter Besant, *As We Are and What We May Be*

In working-class neighbourhoods the street was a far busier and more social place than it is today. There were even sing songs:

> 'At that time singing solo or in small groups as one strolled along the pavement was a daily and welcome feature of working-class life. Broadsheets of popular songs and their parodies were hawked until well into the nineteen twenties, and found ready customers.'
>
> Robert Roberts, *The Classic Slum*

Musicians came round the streets and women and children would come out and dance. In the East End of London Grace Foakes remembered:

> 'Most days in summer and winter we would see the man who played the barrel organ. This was a musical instrument with two wheels and two handles. The man would push it whenever he wanted to play. When he turned the handles it played the popular songs of the day.'
>
> Grace Foakes, *Between High Walls*

MAKING MUSIC

One way for working-class people to listen to music was to make music themselves. Many learnt to play an instrument. The piano was most popular, and some working people managed to afford to buy one. Informal sing songs round the piano were common:

> 'Mum could play from music or by ear. Her chance came when Dad had been quenching his thirst at the local with his mates, and came home a little on the merry side. He would regale all of us with tales of the past, and about his ancestors, and we would all sit round him in the little kitchen till he had unfolded all he could think of. He suddenly decided he would give us a rendering of his "Song and Dance Act". Mum was recruited to provide the background music on the piano. He commenced in the front room with a favourite ditty which had unending verses. The opening bars were "A Fortnight Ago Boys" chorus after chorus rang out, and when they had finished he began his step dance. It's a wonderful thing what a few 2d pints of beer would do. Anyway, these things I have mentioned were enjoyed by all of us in the family.'
>
> John Blake, *Memories of Old Poplar*

Street musicians (1877)

People might play music at work, too. One report on working conditions in London in 1901 notes:

> 'Two girls had been fined for amusing themselves in the dinner-hour by singing and dancing to a small harp in the workroom where they were allowed to remain.'

Musical evenings for friends and neighbours were held in people's front rooms, and local concerts were well attended. This programme for an entertainment at a village hall in the 1870s was typical:

JOHN NEWHAM	**High Kicker**
JOSEPH NEWHAM	**Singer**
MRS HOLYOAKE	**Violin**
THOMAS HOLYOAKE	**Acrobat**
THOMAS NORMAN	**Violin**
JAMES COLVER	**Banjo**
ME	**On the bones**
WILLIAM COLVER	**Stump Oration**

James Hawker, *A Victorian Poacher*

202

FRIENDS AND NEIGHBOURS

For married women working at home, social life was with neighbours — especially in the poorer districts. It seems that the more 'respectable' people were, the more they were likely to 'keep themselves to themselves' and be rather isolated at home:

> 'The slums at any rate have their gossip and common life, but with the advance in the social scale, family life becomes more private and the women, left alone in the house while their husbands are out at work often become mere hopeless drudges.'
>
> R. Nash, 'How the Poor Live', *Investigation Papers, Women's Co-operative Guild 1902*

Maud Pember Reeves described one woman living in Lambeth who had very little social life:

Talking to neighbours (1877)

> 'Mrs O knows nothing of her neighbours and until the visitor insisted on the children getting out every afternoon, Mrs O never took them out. Mr O could not understand why any of his family should ever leave the two rooms where they lived . . . she did her shopping at night in order that her old slippers should not be seen. She sat indoors and mended and made clothes in her neat little room while her pale little girl amused herself as best she could and the baby lay on the bed.'
>
> Maud Pember Reeves, *Round About a Pound a Week*

In contrast to this, life in Poplar, a poorer area, was quite different: 'In the days before the First World War, street doors in every house were always open and were not shut 'til bedtime.' John Blake, *Memories of Old Poplar*

In good weather East End women sat on the front steps to shell their peas or to peel the potatoes and talk to whoever went by. In Islington, Mrs Axham remembers her childhood:

> 'Mother used to love to be out in the front garden and while she was attending to the plants and that, perhaps a neighbour would come by and she used to talk and chat to them.'
>
> Interviewed by Anna Davin

Lady Bell found that the women in Middlesborough visited each others' homes:

> 'The women do go to see one another; you will often find them sitting in each others' houses. More rarely a man who has called to see one of his friends may be found sitting in the latter's house.'
>
> Lady Florence Bell, *At the Works*

In Salford, the local shop was a meeting place for the women, where they shared looking after the children:

> 'If the babies became fretful on Saturday evenings with a shopful of women in for groceries, Mother used to hand them over the counter to be "chain-nursed" by one customer after another, "sometimes for as long as three hours". People came then not only to shop but to talk, the weekly purchase of from one to five shillings worth of goods being a high social occasion. "And if there was any free milk going," my mother used to say, "the babies got it. You've taken nourishment from half the women in the neighbourhood." One customer, a publican's wife, had a copious supply – "mostly milk stout". We came back over the counter then "looking tipsy" and we "always slept well afterwards".'
>
> Robert Roberts, *A Ragged Schooling*

WORKMATES

Many people remember the friendships they made at work:

> 'They used to sing their heads off. Come out singing . . . and you could hear them down the streets with their clogs on, morning after morning. You didn't want an alarm clock. They did go past your house and you did hear them singing, shouting, calling one another, "Alice, come on Alice, it's time to get up." Then you heard the stories of the different women coming into work . . . their struggle and all that.'
>
> Bristol WEA, *Bristol as We Remember It*

Many men remember playing cards or reading the paper in their dinner hour, while women might go window-shopping:

> 'The Highgate factory girls made a tour of the immediate neighbourhood and with their poor, flimsy skirts bedraggled and clinging about their ankles and their toes benumbing on the splashy pavement feasted their eyes on the treasures revealed in the shop of the milliner and the gorgeous display of velvets, silks and sealskins on view at the drapery establishment.'
>
> J. Greenwood, *Low Life Deeps*

USEFUL HOBBIES

Growing flowers and vegetables in the garden (1900)

Many married men and women spent their spare time adding to the family income in some way. A man might keep chickens, or grow fruit and vegetables on an allotment. In the country they might go poaching:

> 'We used to ketch these rabbits – and if you took a rabbit home Granny Webb 'ud take the insides off – out of this rabbit – what we used to call gut him – and she'd have a customer for this rabbit and sell it, that tuppence would go in the cup, to buy their shoes.'
>
> Raphael Samuel, 'Quarry Roughs', in Raphael Samuel (ed) *Village Life and Labour*

Some women had sewing machines and made clothes for their children and husbands. In the country they often made their own jams and pickles from the produce of their gardens:

> 'You never bought vegetables, you kept a chicken or a pig, you made everything yourself you see, you had your fruit, you made your jam, your pickles, and I suppose that's how we did get by.'
>
> Raphael Samuel, 'Quarry Roughs'

READING

Most working-class homes had a 1d (½p) Sunday paper and perhaps a ½d (¼p) local evening paper too. *The News of the World* was the most popular, as was the weekly *Police News* which featured sensational murder stories like that of Jack the Ripper. There were also comics, racing papers and magazines. When Lady Bell made a survey of the reading habits of people in Middlesborough she found:

> 'The working men's wives read less than their husbands. They have no definite intervals of leisure and not so many of them care to read. Twice as many men as women were able to read. Nearly all of them seem to have a feeling that it is wrong to sit down with a book if there is anything more practical to do . . . the men feel amply justified in "sitting down with a book".'
>
> Lady Florence Bell, *At the Works*

Joseph Ashby remembered the same in the country:

> 'Sometimes the girls would feel that fate did not deal evenhandedly between the two sexes. Father and brothers when dark fell or the weather was stormy could sit reading newspapers and books, but if mother sat it was to darn or patch.'
>
> M. Ashby, *Joseph Ashby of Tysoe*

Often people read aloud. At home, women would sew while being read to. At work someone who was good at reading might read the papers aloud to the rest. But it was usually the man who had the monopoly of the newspapers:

> 'He'd pick up the newspaper at night and read it as quick as he could. Nobody would get the paper 'til he had read it. There were two papers on Sunday. He would read one and sit on the other.'
> Terence Monaghan, *Hello Are You Working?*

There were some free public libraries, but sometimes they were not open to women — for example, the miners' libraries in South Wales. Neville Cardus remembered how, in Manchester, 'After working all day in an insurance office 9.30 till 5.00 I went home and had a quick tea. Then off to Dickenson Road library: boys only, girls weren't allowed in.' *(Guardian, 1976)*

POLITICS AND MEETINGS

During the 1880s and 90s there were more political activities involving working people's spare time, such as trades unions, and socialist meetings. The Clarion Club was a socialist group that organised weekend rambles and cycling tours, as well as political meetings. It was especially attractive to young people:

> 'It was a great treat to go on rambles studying botany, geology, economics etc. There was real comradeship. I met Mr Scott at a Cinderella Treat, we were both kneeling, melting butter for the tea and got talking afterwards.'
> Mrs Scott, 'A Felt Hat Worker',
> in Margaret Llewelyn Davies (ed) *Life As We Have Known It*

However, socialist meetings might mean different things to men and women, as Hannah Mitchell found:

> 'Even my Sunday leisure was gone, for I soon found that a lot of the socialist talk about freedom was only talk and these socialist young men expected Sunday dinners and huge teas with home-made cakes, potted meat and pies, exactly like their reactionary fellows. They expected that the girl who had shared their weekend cycling or rambling, summer games or winter dances, would change all her ways with her marriage ring and begin where their mothers left off.'
> Hannah Mitchell, *The Hard Way Up*

Not only was politics traditionally a man's world, but it was very hard for married women with families to attend meetings. Only the most determined or the unmarried managed it. The Women's Co-operative Guild, an organisation for working women, was founded in 1883. It enabled many women

207

to have an independent life outside the home and helped them to get an education. To many members the Guild meant a great deal. But it wasn't always easy to find the time or money:

> 'I was asked to join but told them I could not as I was far too busy. I thought a meeting in the middle of the week was quite impossible. I still had to wash and iron for my living . . . I attended nearly all the Guild conferences, which were often held on a Thursday, the end of my financial week. I have walked six miles to a conference and back because I had no money to pay the fares.'
>
> Mrs Layton, 'Memories of Seventy Years',
> in Margaret Llewelyn Davies (ed) *Life As We Have Known It*

Hannah Mitchell became a Poor Law Guardian, which meant going to meetings during the daytime. She was married with a small child and only managed to attend the meetings because she had a good neighbour who came in to cook the dinner, and by getting up at the crack of dawn to get everything ready. She baked all her own bread, did all the housework, and worked at sewing. Yet she became very active in the campaign for women's votes. It wasn't so hard for a man who wanted to attend meetings, at least in the evenings when his day's work was over. And even the most supportive husband might sometimes feel resentful of his wife's independence:

> 'Sometimes my husband rather resented the teachings of the Guild. The fact that I was determined to assert my right to have the house in my name was a charge against the Guild. The Guild, he said, was making women think too much of themselves.'
>
> Mrs Layton, 'Memories of Seventy Years',
> in Margaret Llewelyn Davies (ed) *Life As We Have Known It*

SOCIAL CLUBS

There were also local social clubs for men and women — though usually separate for the two sexes. Working men's clubs put on entertainments, provided drinks and allowed members to take their wives. Clubs for working women were usually a more sober affair:

> 'I got a big double-fronted shop and had it decorated for them. They'd never seen anything like it before as a social club. They were both married and single and I got them really interested. They were taught Morris and classical dancing. I organised refreshments — tea and cakes at 2d [1p] a time. It was packed.'
>
> Jessie Stephens, trade union organiser

There were public dance halls, but while it was all right for men to go, it was considered rather improper for women, as a female clerk explained:

'Yes, I often go to Caldwell's, there's no harm in that, but still I don't think our firm would think so well of me if they knew; and sometimes, yes, I do meet the gentlemen clerks there and then I have to get them not to mention it.'

Derek Hudson, *Munby, Man of Two Worlds*

SUNDAYS

Many working people didn't get a Saturday half day until this century, so Sunday was their only day off. Many men would spend the day lying on the bed reading the papers, but for women Sunday could mean more work than usual:

'My mother did not have much pleasure but I do not remember her ever complaining – except on Sunday afternoons when father would undress and get into bed, leaving her to mend his working clothes while he had a rest.'

Grace Foakes, *Between High Walls*

One reason for this habit was that often working men only had one set of clothes so they stayed in bed while these were washed.

Life was easier for a woman without children, but there were still jobs to do:

'Polly was 20 and had been married 7 months to a sober chap who only drank beer once a week for his Saturday dinner. On Sunday her chap gave her a cup of tea in bed at seven o'clock, and then she got up and got breakfast. She spent the morning tidying up. "My chap says I'll die with a broom in me 'and," she said. Then she got dinner, generally a meat stew. After dinner she had a "lay down" while her chap read his paper, the weather being too cold to go out.'

Alys Russell, 'Four Days in a Factory', *Contemporary Review, 1903*

Going to church was more common in the country and among the middle classes than for working people in the towns. Many parents sent their children to Sunday school or church though, probably as much for a bit of peace and quiet as anything. Sunday walks to the park and visits to grandparents and aunts took up the afternoons.

Going out meant wearing 'Sunday best' for anyone who could possibly afford it. Grace Foakes remembers how she had to change three times a day in order to keep her best clothes clean:

'Kathleen and I each had one best dress which was kept only for Sundays. We wore them to Sunday school in the morning and on coming home it was taken off until it was time to set out for the afternoon session, when it would go on again. Returning home it would be taken off yet again until the evening lantern service. We had one pair of black stockings each, of a very poor quality. If they were washed too often they took on a greenish hue, so we had to take these off as well when we were not at church.'

Grace Foakes, Between High Walls

A DAY OUT

In the 1880s a week's holiday and even regular days out were beyond the reach of most people. The main outings were the Bank Holidays – Easter, Whit Monday and August. City people went to fairs, pleasure gardens or perhaps a trip to the country or seaside. Londoners could go to Southend by steamer for 3s 6d (17½p). In the country there were traditional celebrations too, like the annual fair, harvest supper and May Day.

Men were more likely to go on an organised outing than women. Grace Foakes described the local 'Beano' for men only:

'Each year in summer every public house in our community would have its annual outing, known as the "Beano". All the year the men would pay into the "Beano club". Then, when the day came, there

A day out in Epping Forest (1880s)

would be enough money for the treat. This was for men only and it was always held on a Sunday.

About eight o'clock we would all gather to watch for the brake. All the men came dressed in their best clothes. Each would have his packet of sandwiches tied with a bright red or green handkerchief. Crates of beer would be loaded into the brake as soon as it arrived, and the men would climb in. The driver would get into his dickey seat and with him came the man who sat next to the driver and who always carried a cornet. When all was ready he would sound a loud fanfare . . . About eleven at night we would hear the sound of the cornet player as the men returned. Most of them were drunk, but they sang and laughed as they set off coloured lights. All declared next day that they had had a wonderful time.'

Grace Foakes, *Between High Walls*

For women and children the annual break was often a working holiday, often hop- or fruit-picking:

'Every year, in the second week in September, many people went hop-picking. Mostly they were women and children; men only went if they happened to be out of work at the time. Nearly all of them went to the Kent hop fields. It was a working holiday but it meant a change of surroundings, fresh air and freedom to enjoy the evenings when the day's work was finished.

We would watch them as they went by. The things they took with them would astound you. They took pots and pans, bedding, toys, carts, prams and pushchairs loaded with every possible thing which they might need, for they stayed six weeks. Nothing was provided for them except a truss of straw to lie on.

They slept in barns, outhouses or huts and all day they would pick hops. When meal times came there was usually a Granny who could not pick but could do the cooking. A fire would have to be made in the open and the meal cooked on this. Sticks and twigs would be gathered for the fire, and water carried from a well. There were no sanitary arrangements except a bucket in a hut. It was a very rough life but these people were tough and knew how to rough it and enjoy it as well.'

Grace Foakes, *Between High Walls*

DRESSING UP

Part of the fun of going out is dressing up, even for the hard up. For ordinary women, fashionable dress at the end of the last century was a long dress, boots, and a hat trimmed with huge feathers:

211

> 'Magenta, orange and royal blue velvet dresses, and huge hats with ostrich feathers of equally flaming hues. It made you quite hot to look at them and they must have suffered to be beautiful on stifling summer days.'
>
> Dorothy MaCall, *When That I Was*

For young men the equivalent in fashion was a bright silk handkerchief or neckscarf, waistcoat and a cap.

Make-up which had, until now, mainly been used by prostitutes, was just beginning to become popular, although lipstick was unheard of until the beginning of this century. A women's magazine reported:

> 'Make-up seems to become almost a passion for most women who indulge in it to any extent. There is little room for doubt that the "art" is on the increase. A chemist only the other day remarked to me how much the practice has grown of late. "Quite young girls come in now," he said, "and ask for powder, rouge, eyebrow pencils and kohl, without the least embarrassment." '
>
> 'The Art of Beauty' 1899

Curly fringes were all the rage too:

> 'When I got taken on in the factory 44 out of the 45 girls employed there wore these curlers and many of them told me that they kept them on from Monday morning until Saturday afternoon when they burst forth, I suppose, in the glory of a really curly fringe.'
>
> Alys Russell, 'Four Days in a Factory', *Contemporary Review, 1903*

TIME AND MONEY

Leisure was a completely different matter for the very rich, and different again for those with enough to spare for modest luxuries. There were all sorts of new leisure pursuits by the end of the century for anyone who could afford them. There were holidays by rail to the seaside; easier travel to Europe, perhaps taking one of Thomas Cook's tours; motoring to the city or country — the cheapest car was £200 in the 1890s: a bicycle — £30 for a good model. The benefits of electricity, telephones, the combustion engine were all felt by the better-off, but hardly touched the lives of the majority of people before this century.

The separation of men's and women's activities was even more marked among the wealthier classes. With both time and money available, they were more likely to follow the rules of 'correct' behaviour which largely restricted women to the home.

Men had their gentlemen's clubs where they could meet to discuss politics, drink, smoke and gamble — the equivalent of the working man's pub. At weekends there was hunting, shooting or the new sports of polo and golf (more expensive and exclusive than going to watch football). If a gentleman owned a motorcar, his wife might have to be very long-suffering, as the diary of Mrs Koosen, written in 1895, reveals:

Nov 23	Took train to Lee and tried to make our motor work; wouldn't. Came home at five.
Nov 24	Awfully cold; played with our motor — no result.
Nov 25	After lunch saw to our motor, but didn't get it out of shed.
Nov 26	Drove to Lee and took Smith and Penning (engineers). Penning spent the day on his back without results.
Nov 30	Motor went with benzoline for first time; awfully pleased.
Dec 2	Waiting for new oil.
Dec 9	Drove to Lee at ten. Motor sparked at once and went well. After lunch started for home in motor car; came round by Fareham; had lovely drive; police spotted us; awful crowd followed us at Cosham; had to beat them off with umbrella.
Dec 10	Policeman called at 10.30, took our names re driving through Fareham without red flag ahead.
Dec 27	Frightened an unattended horse attached to a milkcart, which bolted and sent the milk cans flying in all directions.
Jan 4	Lost nut off air valve; pushed home.

MANNERS AND RULES

For the comfortably-off or the well-to-do woman at home, social life centred on 'visiting'. As well as keeping company with other women it was also important to establish suitable social contacts for her husband, which might lead to business promotion, and for her children to ensure good marriages. Great importance was attached to following the correct rules of etiquette. Here is the procedure for leaving visiting cards:

> 'Leaving cards is the first step towards forming or enlarging a circle of acquaintances. Leaving cards principally devolves upon the mistress of the house. A wife should leave cards for her husband as well as herself. Mostly cards should be delivered in person, and not sent by post. A lady should desire her man servant to enquire if the mistress of the house at which she is calling is "at home". If "not at home" she should hand him three cards; one of her own, and two of her husband's; her card is left for the mistress of the house and her husband's for both master and mistress.'
>
> *Manners and Rules of Good Society*, 1888

Surprisingly enough, morning calls were made in the afternoon, from three to four if formal, from four to five if semi-formal, and from five to six if to good friends. Calls were supposed to be strictly limited to fifteen minutes of polite conversation and busy women might get to three or four houses in a day. A considerable amount of time was spent each day changing clothes in order to be 'correctly' dressed for every occasion. The only exercise was 'carriage exercise', which meant going for a drive. Dinner parties were held in the evenings, and there were different rules for ladies and gentlemen:

> 'Ladies are not supposed to require a second glass of wine at dessert, and passing the decanters is principally for the gentlemen. If a lady should require a second glass of wine at dessert, the gentleman seated next to her should fill her glass; she should not help herself to wine.'
>
> 'As a matter of course young ladies do not eat cheese at dinner parties.'
>
> *Manners and Rules of Good Society*, 1888

After the meal they each went their separate ways:

> 'At the right moment when the supper was done she rose magnificently and signalled to the ladies in absolutely the correct manner. They retired to the parlour. They left the gentlemen to port and cheroots and their dirty stories . . . The ladies arranged themselves about the freshly anti-macassared parlour, and the chat turned to local matters. There was always some amusing gossip going on the

214

rounds which ravished the ladies. What the gentlemen said and did
was well shut away.'

Ursula Bloom, Requesting The Pleasure

By the 1900s wealthy women were just beginning to smoke in their own homes. It was considered rather daring to do it in front of men, and certainly it wasn't done in public.

'THE NEW WOMAN'

During the 1880s and 90s more and more women in the upper and middle classes were starting to break away from this restricted social life — by joining in active sports and becoming involved in politics for example. They were labelled 'The New Woman'. Molly Hughes described a friend of hers:

'She certainly typified the modern girl of that time, tame though it may seem to us today. She had been long before this one of the first women to ride a bicycle, to go on the top of a bus, and to indulge in mixed bathing.'

Molly Hughes, A London Girl of the 1880s

It was a sign of the times that the Ladies Sanitary Association campaigned for the provision of public lavatories for women; until then, women hadn't gone out for long enough periods to make this necessary!

'No longer in these days, confined to the limits of their hearth, or at any rate to short and easy journeys within the circle of their immediate neighbourhoods, they have now to traverse the great and crowded thoroughfares of towns and remain absent from home for hours on errands of importance to themselves and their families.'

Ladies Sanitary Association Report, 1880s

Mixed sports like archery and tennis became popular, although at first women were ridiculously hindered by their clothes. In 1893 for example, they were advised to wear long woollen dresses for tennis:

'Wool should in some measure form the material, for health's sake, as a preventive of chills being taken; therefore cashmere, serge, and flannel are chosen. The bodice is usually made full, and the skirt is short [ankle length] and not burdened with many frills and flounces . . . a receptacle for the tennis balls is sometimes part of the player's costume . . . Hats of every variety are worn.'

Etiquette of Good Society, 1893

Bicycling became very popular with both men and women. It offered women a new freedom, as one cyclist explained:

'There is a new dawn, a dawn of emancipation, and it is brought about by the cycle. Free to wheel, free to spin into the glorious country unhampered by chaperone or even dispiriting male admirers, the young girl of today can feel the real independence of herself.'

Louise Jey, 1895

At first, women on bikes created a sensation. They were sometimes even pulled off by bystanders who thought it an amusing sight; while ladies' magazines warned of the dangers:

'The mere act of riding a bicycle is not in itself sinful and if it is the only way of reaching the church on Sunday it may be excusable. On the other hand, if walking or riding in the usual way is discarded for the sake of the exercise or exhilaration bicycle riding affords, it is clearly wrong.'

Home Companion, 1885

One important result of the craze for sports and exercise was that tight-lacing and eighteen inch waists went out of fashion and looser, more comfortable clothes were becoming acceptable and fashionable by the end of the century.

WOMEN'S RIGHTS

The growing concern with poverty in the 1880s and 90s meant that there were increasing opportunities to do voluntary and social work or to become involved in local government. Women in particular became involved, for if they were from the better-off classes they had plenty of time and welcomed the chance to do something useful.

In the 1880s Octavia Hill, for example, worked to improve housing in the East End of London; Beatrice Webb worked on social investigations among the poor with Charles Booth; Catherine Booth, with her husband William, founded and ran the Salvation Army from 1875 onwards. And there were many more who were involved in similar activities without becoming famous.

Probably the best-known women at this time were the suffragettes who, with the suffragists (who used different tactics), campaigned for women's right to vote. At the beginning of this century, when their campaign became a militant one, many of them suffered imprisonment and forced feeding when they went on hunger strike for their beliefs, and they fought a tremendous battle against the government, which went on for many years. Many – though by no means all – the women who fought for the vote, could have been leading leisurely lives. The suffragette movement, because of its importance, has been written about many times already. Here is an account of one woman's personal contribution.

Leonora Cohen, a suffragette from Leeds (1873–1978) hit the headlines for her protest at the Tower of London. She talked in 1977 at the age of 104, about what happened:

'It got a lot of publicity – I can remember when I was bailed out the press called it "Raid on the Tower of London". I bought a guide to find out what to do and when I told the lady I was staying with she said, "You'll never get into the Tower – you'll never do it!"

It was a Saturday morning. When I got on the Underground she told me where to get off and I was so agitated I was nearly fainting. I just couldn't get up – the use of my legs had gone. Then I thought to myself, "Oh, it's Saturday morning – they'll be closing," so with a supreme effort I followed a school party that was just going in.

At the door I bought some postcards and then I followed this crocodile. We went into the Jewel House and it was full. I threw the iron bar I had at the glass. The place was cleared in a minute. Of course, I had a good aim. I had had a look to see where I could aim and being tall I went for the glass case containing the Orders of Merit of the British Empire. Air raids during the war were nothing to me after doing that!

I was arrested and taken to Leman Street police station, and from

Leonora Cohen, in her eighties, revisiting the Tower of London

there to the Thames police. They put me in a filthy cell and brought the superintendant. He said "Have I seen you before?" I answered him, "It isn't for me to tell you, you should know."

The message I had written and tied with a ribbon to the iron bar was: "This is my protest to the government's treachery to the working women of Great Britain." '

EQUAL OPPORTUNITIES

The suffragette movement eventually won the struggle for the right of women to vote. In 1918, after having played a crucial role in running industry and the public services during the First World War women at the age of thirty, but all men at twenty-one were given the right to vote, and women could stand as parliamentary candidates. Not until 1928 did women win equal rights with men to vote at twenty-one.

Since then women have gradually come to play a greater part in political life, although there are still only a tiny number of women MPs in the House of Commons. Certain hard-fought-for legal rights have been won too, such as the Equal Pay and Sex Discrimination Acts of 1975. There is less restriction now on women's social lives. For example, there are women's sports teams; women can go out with other women to entertainments, bars and restaurants without criticism; and smaller families and greater financial independence have meant that women have more opportunity for leisure.

However, as in the other areas of life examined in this book, in some ways change has not been so very great. The pub is still a predominantly male institution, with no female equivalent; many women are still tied to the home to a greater extent than men by children and domestic responsibilities; in many city areas women feel restricted from going out at night from fear of violence from men.

The Equal Opportunities Commission has pinpointed the need to go much further than simply making new laws to bring about real equality of opportunity:

'The Sex Discrimination Act cannot remove all the influence of tradition, custom and prejudice . . . If equality of opportunity is to become a reality the application of the letter of the law is not sufficient. The spirit underlying the legislation has to be absorbed by all concerned . . . and it is the responsibility of the Equal Opportunities Commission to raise the consciousness of everyone involved and to ensure that both sexes receive equal treatment.'

'Do You Provide Equal Opportunities?',
Equal Opportunities Commission

QUESTIONS

The pub p. 194:

1. According to Flora Thompson's account, what were the attractions of the pub for the men of Forlow? Why do you think the women did not go?

2. The two extracts on page 196 describe women going into pubs in London. Why do you think London might have been different from the country?

Spending money p. 196:

3. How was spending money for the single woman different from men's? Why do you think the married women had no spending money? How did they manage to pay for treats, according to Maud Pember Reeves?

A night out p. 197:

4. Why do you think there were more men and boys than women in the music hall audience described here? Is this still the case in any place of entertainment today?

Sport and gambling p. 199:

5 Why do you think only men played sport? How far do women take as great an interest and play as great a part as men in sport today?

On the streets p. 200:

6. Why do you think the street was a centre of social life? Where do people meet up today?

Making music p. 201:

7. What has replaced the piano in people's homes today, and why?

Friends and neighbours p. 203:

8. Why do you think the people described by R. Nash and Maud Pember Reeves 'kept themselves to themselves', while those described by John Blake and Mrs Axham behaved differently? How does social class affect neighbourliness today?

9. Why do you think the women visited each other's homes far more than the men, as described by Lady Bell? Is this true today?

Useful hobbies p. 205 and Reading p. 206:

10. What 'useful' hobbies do men and women have today? Do you think men and women are less divided in their interests than in the past?

11. Why did the women described in these extracts read less than men? Is this still the case? Do men and women read different things? Who reads newspapers most today?

Politics and meetings p. 207:

12.   Why did Hannah Mitchell object to the men's attitude? Does this happen today?

13.   Is it easier today for women to be involved in politics and meetings? Why did Mrs Layton's husband sometimes resent the teachings of the Guild? Do men sometimes resent women's independence today, or do you think attitudes have changed?

Social clubs p. 208:

14.   Why was it all right for men, but not for women, to go to dance halls? Are there any places today where it is acceptable for men to go but not for women?

Sundays p. 209:

15.   Why did women have to work on Sundays? Who works more on Sundays today, either in the home or for money, men or women?

A day out p. 210:

16.   What do you think the men enjoyed about the 'Beano'? What were the attractions of hop-picking for women? Do either of these kinds of activities go on today?

Time and money p. 212:

17.   What does the diary tell us about early motoring? And about the first motorists?

Manners and rules p. 214:

18.   From the evidence here, in what ways was upper-class social life different from that of the working classes? How do class differences affect social life today?

19.   Are there different rules and manners for men and women today? What do you think the reasons were for the differences described here?

'The New Woman' p. 215:

20.   Why do you think there were such strong objections to women riding bikes? What sorts of behaviour or clothes cause outrage today? Try to find out from older people what was considered outrageous ten or fifteen years ago.

Women's rights p. 216:

21.   What do you think of Leonora Cohen's protest? Do you admire her or not?

Equal opportunities p. 218:

22.   Do you think men and women today have the same amount of spare time? Do they have equal opportunities to spend it as they wish?

Conclusion

The process of change as a whole over the last century shows a number of contradictions. First, there have been enormous changes in some aspects of everyday life. Perhaps the most important has been the effect of contraception, both on women's lives and health and on marriage and family life for both women and men. Most people can now choose and control the number of children they have. The standard of health too has changed greatly. In Britain, babies no longer commonly die from minor infections; adults rarely die of TB as they did in large numbers in the last century.

However, even where progress has been made, there are still many unsolved problems and unanswered questions. We still have no completely safe, satisfactory and reliable form of birth control. Many diseases have still not been conquered, and many people still live and work in conditions that are dangerous to their health.

Change has not always been for the better either. For instance, women have not gained greater opportunities to work equally with men when and if they choose with any steady progress. Openings for women's employment have depended on the state of the economy generally; during both world wars women were encouraged to work outside the home, as they were during the financial boom of the sixties. After each war, and during the recessions of the 1930s and 80s women have been laid off first and encouraged to return to the home, regardless of their own economic or personal

221

need to work. The same applies to child care facilities. During the last war there were government-run crêches and nurseries to enable women to work. Now these facilities are regarded as a luxury the country cannot afford.

In contrast to some vast changes such as family size or life expectancy, there are some aspects of life that have changed amazingly little, if at all. In spite of the so-called sexual revolution, sex education is still extremely limited, and ignorance is still widespread — as illustrated by the high number of unwanted pregnancies each year. And, in spite of over a century of trades unionism many workers still have to put up with poor conditions, low pay and few rights. While the women's liberation movement has raised important issues, women still do most of the shopping, cleaning, cooking and child care that keep our homes functioning.

Attitudes in particular change very slowly and illustrate the contradictions in the process of change. For example, certain jobs are still considered unsuitable for women, but not for men, because they involve physical exertion or danger or command authority. The education system still channels girls and boys into traditionally 'female' and 'male' subject areas, in spite of the theory (and to some extent the practice) of equal opportunities. And regardless of what women have achieved and fought for in proving their capabilities, they are very often presented by the media as sexy and decorative rather than competent and decisive like men.

The concept of difference also requires careful consideration. While the last century has brought about an overall higher standard of living in Britain, there has been far less change in the huge difference between rich and poor. If anything, the gulf has become wider, since a smaller number of people than before now own most of the wealth in this country. In practical terms this means that the quality of health care, education, diet, housing, daily domestic life, leisure facilities and many other aspects of life still depend on class to a considerable extent. Radio, TV, holidays and new clothes are no longer luxuries, but in the 1980s, as in the 1880s, roughly one-third of the population exists on or below the bare minimum wage necessary for any kind of reasonable survival. And although there may be greater equality between the sexes than before, there are still great differences between how men and women experience their lives.

It is important to discover and record the history of women and men. Ordinary people of all classes and both sexes are part of history and, in living their lives, make history.

Sources quoted

Most of these books are easily found in public libraries. The editions given are, wherever possible, the most recent.

Anon, *Manners and Rules of Good Society* Frederick Warne, 1888

Ashby, Mabel, *Joseph Ashby of Tysoe, 1859–1919* Cambridge University Press, 1961

Barnes, Ron, *Coronation Cups and Jam Jars* Centerprise, 1976

Beeton, Isobel, *Book of Household Management* (first published 1861) Jonathan Cape, 1968

Bell, Florence, *At the Works* Edward Arnold, 1907

Besant, Walter, *As We Are and What We May Be* Chatto and Windus, 1903

Blake, John, *Memories of Old Poplar* Stepney Books, 1978

Bloom, Ursula, *Requesting the Pleasure* Robert Hale, 1973

Booth, Charles, *Life and Labour of the People of London* Macmillan, 1902–3

Booth, William, *In Darkest England and the Way Out* Salvation Army, 1890

Bristol WEA, *Bristol as We Remember It* Bristol Broadsides, 1977

Brittain, Vera, *Testament of Youth*, (first published 1931) Virago 1978

Bulley & Whitley, *Women's Work* Methuen, 1894

Burnett, John (ed), *Useful Toil* Allen Lane, 1974

Ellis, Sarah, *Women of England* Fisher & Co, 1838

Foakes, Grace, *Between High Walls* Pergamon, 1974

Foakes, Grace, *My Part of the River* Futura, 1976

Gilman Perkins, Charlotte, *The Yellow Wallpaper* (first published 1892) Virago Press, 1981

Greenwood, James, *Low Life Deeps* London, 1877

Griffiths, Neil, *Shops Book, Brighton 1900–1930* Queen Spark Books, Brighton, 1979

Hackney WEA, *The Threepenny Doctor* Centerprise, 1974

Hackney WEA, *Working Lives* Centerprise, 1974

Hall, Ruth, *Marie Stopes* Virago Press, 1978

Hall, Ruth (ed), *Dear Dr Stopes* André Deutsch, 1978

Hardy, Thomas, *Tess of the D'Urbervilles* (first published 1891) Penguin, 1978

Hawker James (ed Garth Christian), *A Victorian Poacher* OUP, 1978

Hudson, Derek, *Munby, Man of Two Worlds* John Murray, 1972

Hughes, Molly, *A London Child of the 1870s* OUP, 1977

Hughes, Molly, *A London Girl of the 1880s* OUP, 1977

Jeffries, Richard, *Field and Hedgerow* London, 1899

Karsland, Vera, *Women and their Work* Sampson Low, 1891

Kilvert, Francis, *Kilvert's Diary 1870–1879* Penguin, 1977

Langley, John, *Always a Layman* Queen Spark Books, Brighton, 1976

Lewis, Taffy, *Any Road* Trinity Arts, Birmingham 1979

Llewelyn Davies, Margaret (ed), *Life As We Have Known It* by Co-operative working women (first published 1931) Virago Press, 1977

Llewelyn Davies, Margaret (ed), *Maternity, Letters from Working Women* (first published 1915) Virago Press, 1978

MacCall, Dorothy, *When That I Was* Faber, 1952

Marcus, Stephen, *The Other Victorians* Corgi, 1969

Maugham, Somerset, *Of Human Bondage* (first published 1915) Heinemann, 1937

Mayhew, Henry, *London Labour and the London Poor* Griffin, Bohn & Co, 1861

Mitchell, Hannah, *The Hard Way Up* Virago Press, 1977

Monaghan, Terence, *Hello Are You Working?* Strong Words, Whitley Bay, 1977

Moore, George, *Esther Waters* Walter Scott, 1894

Newton, Arthur, *Years of Change* Hackney WEA & Centerprise, 1974

Noakes, George, *To be a Farmer's Boy* Queen Spark Books, Brighton, 1977

Paterson, Alexander, *Across the Bridges* London, 1911

Paul, Albert, *Poverty, Hardship but Happiness* Queen Spark Books, Brighton, 1974

Pember Reeves, Maud, *Round About a Pound a Week* (first published 1913) Virago Press, 1979

Petrie, Glen, *A Singular Iniquity – The Campaigns of Josephine Butler* Macmillan, 1971

Powell, Margaret, *Below Stairs* Pan, 1970

Roberts, Elizabeth, 'Working Class Women in the North West' in *Oral History* 1977 vol.5, no.2 Oral History Society

Roberts, Robert, *A Ragged Schooling* Fontana/Collins, 1978

Roberts, Robert, *The Classic Slum* Pelican, 1973

Rook, Clarence, *The Hooligan Nights* (first published 1899) OUP, 1979

Rowntree, Seebohm, *Poverty: A Study in Town Life* (first published 1901) Howard Fertig, New York, 1971

Royston Pike, E., *Human Documents of the Age of the Forsytes* Allen & Unwin, 1969

Russell, Alys, 'Four Days in a Factory' in *Contemporary Review*, 1903

Russell, Dora, *The Tamarisk Tree* Virago Press, 1977

Samuel, Raphael (ed), *Miners, Quarrymen and Saltworkers* Routledge & Kegan Paul, 1977

Samuel, Raphael (ed), *Village Life and Labour* Routledge & Kegan Paul, 1975

Sims, George, *How the Poor Live* Chatto & Windus, 1883

Spalding, T.H., *The Work of the London School Board* London 1900

Spring-Rice, Margery, *Working Class Wives* (first published 1939) Virago Press, 1980

Stopes, Marie, *Married Love* Fifield, 1918

Stopes, Marie, *The First Five Thousand* John Ball, 1925

Strachey, Ray, *The Cause* (first published 1928) Virago Press, 1978

Thompson, Flora, *Lark Rise to Candleford* Penguin, 1973

Thompson, Paul, 'The War with Adults' in *Oral History 1975* vol.3 no.2 Oral History Society

Vigne, Thea, 'Parents and Children 1890–1918 – Distance & Dependence' in *Oral History 1975* vol.3 no.2 Oral History Society

Walsh, Jane, *Not Like This* Lawrence & Wishart, 1953

Yonge, Charlotte, *Womankind* Mosley & Smith, 1876

Suggestions for further reading

The following books are accessible and contain useful source material and extracts.

GENERAL

Adams, Carol & Lavrikietis, Rae *The Gender Trap* Quartet 1980 (2nd ed)
Bristol Women's Study Group, *Half the Sky* Virago Press, 1979
Crowther, Nicci, *I Can Remember* Edward Arnold, 1976
Rowbotham, Sheila, *Hidden from History* Pluto, 1973
Rowbotham, Sheila & McCrindle, Jean (eds), *Dutiful Daughters* Pelican, 1979
Thompson, Paul & Harkell, Gina, *The Edwardians in Photographs* Batsford, 1979

GROWING UP

Allen, Eleanor, *Victorian Children* A & C Black, 1979
Bristol WEA, 1977 *Bristol Childhood* Bristol Broadsides
Bristol WEA, 1979 *Looking Back on Bristol* Bristol Broadsides
Bristol WEA, 1979 *Up Knowle West* Bristol Broadsides
Elias, Eileen, *On Sundays We Wore White* Robin Clark, 1980
Fyson, Lui Nance, *Growing Up in Edwardian Britain* Batsford, 1980
Horn, Pamela, *The Victorian Country Child* Roundwood Press, 1974
Jasper, A.S., *A Hoxton Childhood* Centerprise, 1973
Plowden, Alison, *The Case of Eliza Armstrong* BBC Publications, 1974
Thompson, Thea, *Edwardian Childhoods* Routledge & Kegan Paul, 1981

GETTING AN EDUCATION

Horn, Pamela, *Education in Rural England 1800–1914* Gill & Macmillan 1978

Kamm, Josephine, *Hope Deferred: Girls' Education in English History* Methuen, 1965

McCann, Philip (ed), *Popular Education and Socialisation in the 19th Century* Methuen, 1977

Widdowson, Frances, *Going up into the Next Class* Women's Research & Resources Centre, 1981

EARNING A LIVING

Bagnold, Enid, *A Diary Without Dates* Virago Press, 1978

Hall, Edith, *Canary Girls and Stockpots* Luton WEA, 1977

Hiley, Michael, *Victorian Working Women: Portraits from Life* Gordon Fraser, 1979

Holcombe, Lee, *Victorian Ladies at Work* David & Charles, 1973

Hugget, Frank, *A Day in the Life of a Victorian Factory Worker* Allen & Unwin, 1973

Kamm, Josephine, *Rapiers and Battleaxes* Allen & Unwin, 1966

Liddington, Jill & Norris, Jill, *One Hand Tied Behind Us* Virago Press, 1978

Wenzel, Marian & Cornish, John, *Auntie Mabel's War* Allen Lane, 1980

GETTING MARRIED

Adam, Ruth, *A Woman's Place: 1910–75* Chatto & Windus 1975

Forrester, Wendy, *Great Grandmama's Weekly Girls' Own Paper 1880–1901* Lutterworth, 1980

Hughes, Molly, *A London Home in the 1890s* OUP, 1978

Maugham, Somerset, *Liza of Lambeth* (first published 1887) Heinemann, 1934

Moore, Katherine, *Victorian Wives* Allison & Busby, 1974

HAVING A FAMILY

Fryer, Peter, *The Birth Controllers* Corgi, 1967

Stopes Roe, Harry & Scott, Ian, *Marie Stopes and Birth Control* Priory Press, 1975

RUNNING THE HOME

Allen, Eleanor, *Home Sweet Home: A History of Housework* A & C Black, 1979

Davidoff, Leonore & Hawthorn, Ruth, *A Day in the Life of a Victorian Domestic Servant* Allen & Unwin, 1976

Fearn, Jacqueline, *Domestic Bygones* Shire Publications, 1977

Harrison, Molly, *The Kitchen in History* Osprey, 1972

Meadows, Cecil, *The Victorian Ironmonger* Shire Publications, 1978

Noakes, Daisy, *The Town Beehive – a young girl's lot, Brighton 1910–34* Queen Spark Books, Brighton, 1975

KEEPING HEALTHY

Ehrenreich, Barbara & English, Deirdre, *Complaints and Disorders: The sexual politics of sickness* Writers & Readers, 1973

Ehrenreich, Barbara & English, Deirdre, *For Her Own Good: 150 years of the experts' advice to women* Pluto, 1979

IN YOUR SPARE TIME

Davidoff, Leonore, *The Best Circles* Croom Helm, 1973

Dewhirst, Ian, *The Story of a Nobody* Mills & Boon, 1980

Galsworthy, John, *The Forsyte Chronicles* Penguin, 1951

McKenzie, Midge, *Shoulder to Shoulder* Penguin, 1975

Ramelson, Marian, *The Petticoat Rebellion: A century of struggle for women's rights* Lawrence & Wishart, 1972

Willmott Dobbie, B.M., *A Nest of Suffragettes in Somerset* The Batheaston Society, 1979

Bibliographies and Resources

PUBLISHED BIBLIOGRAPHIES

Rowbotham, Sheila, *Women's Liberation and Revolution* Falling Wall Press, 1973

White, Bob, *Non-Sexist Teaching Materials and Approaches* New Childhood Press, 1971

BIBLIOGRAPHIES ON WOMEN IN HISTORY FROM:

London Feminist History Group c/o Women's Research & Resources Centre, 190 Upper Street, London N1.

History & Social Sciences Teachers' Centre, 377 Clapham Road, London SW9.

Library, Goldsmiths' College, Lewisham Way, London SE14.

INFORMATION ON BOOKS FROM:

Equal Opportunities Commission, Overseas House, Quay Street, Manchester M3 3HN.

Fawcett Library, City of London Polytechnic, Calcutta Precinct, Oldcastle Street, London E1.

Sisterwrite Books, 190 Upper Street, London N1.

Virago Press, 41 William IV Street, London WC2N 4DB.

WIRES, Women's Information and Referral Service, 32a Shakespeare Street, Nottingham.

Women in Education, 14 St Brendan's Road, Withington, Manchester 20.

Women's Press, 124 Shoreditch High Street, London E1.

Women's Research & Resources Centre, Hungerford House, Victoria Embankment, London WC2.